Eaves Dropper

Overheard On The Streets

EAVESDROPPER

Overheard On The Streets

By Mete Erdogan

STERLING
New York

STERLING
New York

An Imprint of Sterling Publishing
1166 Avenue of the Americas
New York, NY 10036

ISBN 978-1-4549-1753-3

Distributed in Canada by Sterling Publishing
c/o Canadian Manda Group, 664 Annette Street
Toronto, Ontario, Canada M6S 2C8

Distributed in the United Kingdom
by GMC Distribution Services
Castle Place, 166 High Street,
Lewes, East Sussex, England BN7 1XU

Distributed in Australia
by Capricorn Link (Australia) Pty. Ltd.
P.O. Box 704, Windsor, NSW 2756, Australia

For information about custom editions, special sales,
and premium and corporate purchases, please contact Sterling
Special Sales at 800-805-5489 or
specialsales@sterlingpublishing.com.

Manufactured in China

2   4   6   8   10   9   7   5   3   1

www.sterlingpublishing.com

Thank you to all
who inspired me
during this project.
Both willingly
or unknowingly.

Heard at 'Essen' on Vandam and Varick

I'd rather

be Eating

Heard in the Macy's shoe section

Heard at GameStop, Brooklyn

You gotta *Moisturize* BRO

Heard at Gigino, Wagner Park

Stop asking questions and

GET
ON MY
LEVEL

Heard at Palma, West Village

Heard on South 1st, Brooklyn

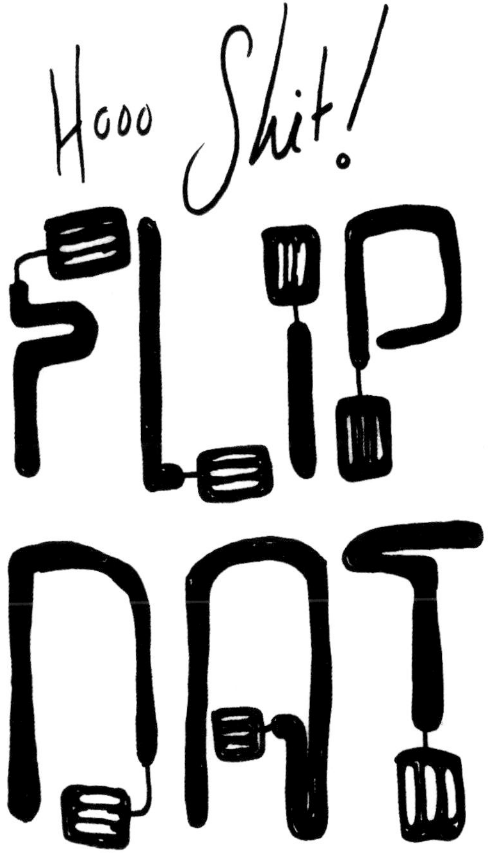
Hooo Shit!
FLIP
DAT

Heard at Mission Cantina, East Village

Heard at Dunkin' Donuts on Hudson and Clarkson

THERE'S SO MUCH GOOD TV NOW.

Heard at Wafels & Dinges, East Village

There's a National "Be Nice" Day?

...Shit. I've missed every year.

Heard at the Big Gay Ice Cream Shop

Heard at Freehold Café, Brooklyn

DON'T THANK ME, THANK DAVID BOWIE.

Heard at Miller's Tavern, Brooklyn

Heard at work

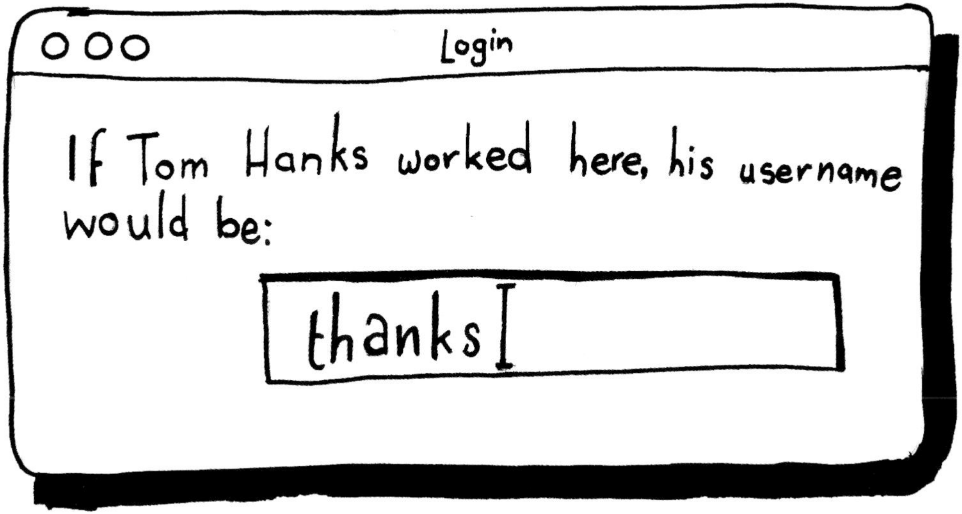
Login
If Tom Hanks worked here, his username would be:
thanks

Heard by my desk

Heard at my desk

I CAN'T EXPLAIN
THE GLITTER IN
MY EARS BUT I
SWEAR I HAVEN'T
BEEN TO A
Strip Club

Heard at Chobani, SoHo

SHE WAS WEARING OVERALLS,
I just assumed
SHE WAS A GOOD PERSON.

Heard at Brooklyn Brewery, Williamsburg

Heard at my desk

Was Martha Stewart the PAMELA ANDERSON of her time?

Heard in the elevator

IT'S NOT *Moderation,* IT'S ABSENCE OF GUILT.

Heard in the office

Heard in a cab in The Meatpacking District

GET IN THE CAR!

I JUST DROVE PAST THIS PARTY AND EVERYONE'S NAKED!

Heard in Bali, Indonesia

Heard at Insomnia Cookies

You can't just survive on Gelato and Desperate Housewives.

Heard at Palma, West Village

I just wanna take my pants off.

Heard at Freehold Café, Brooklyn

Heard on 4th and Ave B, East Village

I'M PROUD OF YOU MOFOS

I didn't know you had a birthmark there!

...Wait... no, it's just lint.

Heard in the East Village

Seen in my Facebook Newsfeed

I CANNOT EVEN...
THE PUMPKIN
SPICE LATTE I HAD
THIS MORNING
WAS LIKE SO RAVEN.

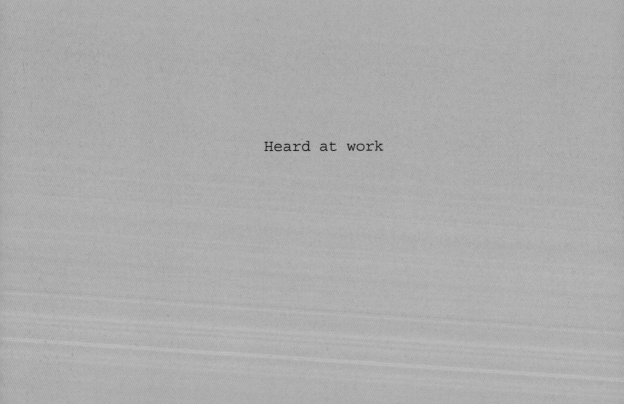

Heard at work

ANYONE

WHO SAYS THERE'S

No Farting

IN YOGA

IS A LIAR!

Heard at Toby's Estate, Brooklyn

Cops & Baristas

PROBABLY SEE PEOPLE
AT THEIR WORST.

YOU'RE ALSO A PET.

Heard on the corner of 4th and Ave B. East Village

Heard in the elevator

Heard at Mission Cantina, East Village

I knew they were meant for each other when they got back together for the third time.

Heard at La Colombe, West Village

Heard by my desk

Heard at work

Heard at work

There is no scent
on this earth
more comforting
than frying onions.

I'm trying to
eat less...

...trying to.

Heard by my desk

Heard in the lobby

ARE YOU WASTED ALREADY?...

WHERE ARE YOU?...

THE PLACE WITH THE CANDLE?...

Heard on the corner of Bedford and Metropolitan, Brooklyn

Heard in the lobby

THERE'S NOTHING WRONG WITH

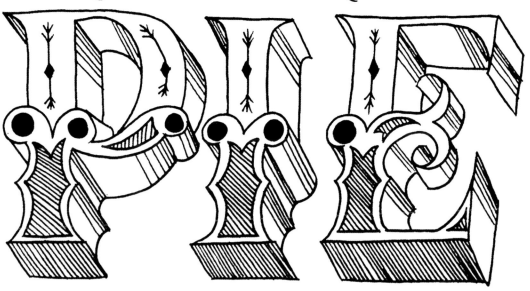

PIE

Heard at Sweatshop, Williamsburg

We Haven't Met, But...

Can I

Touch

your

Dog?

Heard at Westville, West Village

WHY DOES "I'M NOT DRINKING TONIGHT" GET THE SAME REACTION AS "I'M A CAT PERSON"?

Heard by my desk

DO YOU THINK BEYONCÉ CRIES TO HER OWN MUSIC WHEN SHE'S SAD?

Heard in the boardroom

I'm not Evil, I'm Realistic.

Heard at Maialino, East Village

There's no way to look cool on an elliptical machine.

Heard on the corner of Charlton and Varick

DUDE, GET THIS,

"Ellen

Degeneres

GIVES AWAY FREE STUFF

ON HER SHOW ALL THE TIME...

SHE'S ELLEN THE GENEROUS!

Heard at work

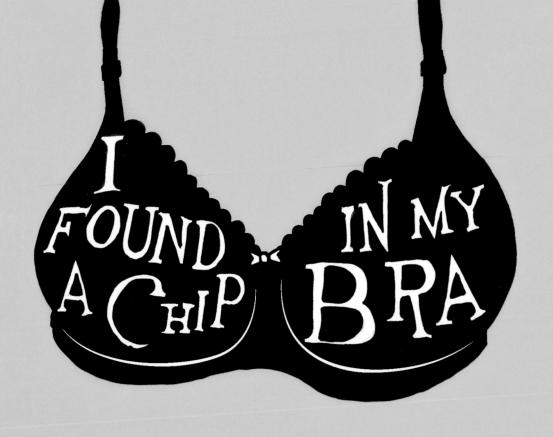

Heard at Sweatshop, Williamsburg

The tattoo on his thumb's gonna wear out from so much swiping on Tinder. :D

Heard at Sweatshop, Williamsburg

...During the same conversation

... *Seriously* though,
it's an ice breaker
and a deal breaker
at the same time.

Heard in the office

SPOONING LEADS TO FORKING.

Heard at the Ace Hotel

that's the funniest thing i've seen since my 14 year old son hit puberty.

Heard on Metropolitan and Bedford

Keys,
Wallet,
Phone.
...Okay, we're good.

I've finally figured
out what women want...

It's grilled cheese... They want grilled cheese

Heard on Powers St, Brooklyn

Heard at work

CRYPIN' AIN'T EASY.

Heard in the East Village

MY FRIEND
SLEPT WITH
BUZZ FROM
HOME ALONE.

you're a beautiful girl,
—you're a kind girl,

but you're an idiot.

Seen in my Facebook newsfeed

Heard on Powers St, Brooklyn

WE COULDN'T BE TOGETHER. YOU DON'T KNOW *parkour.*

Heard in the elevator

I'M ON A LANGUAGE CLEANSE. IT'S LIKE A JUICE CLEANSE BUT YOU CAN'T SAY THINGS LIKE FUCK...

... SHIT

Heard in the elevator

FUCK FASHION, I'M COLD!

Heard at Casey Rubber Stamps

It's Okay,
I'll come back
with someone
who has patience
for my obsession...

Heard at Sweatshop, Williamsburg

Ryan Gosling
is just a better looking
Draco Malfoy.

Heard at work

Heard at Sweatshop, Williamsburg

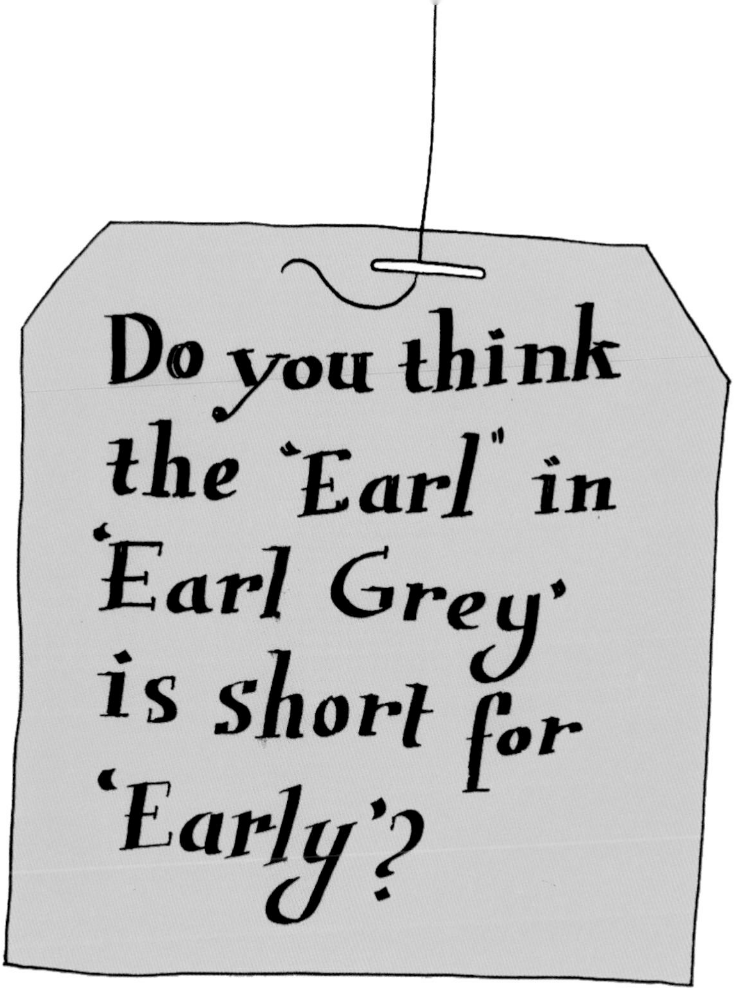
Do you think the "Earl" in 'Earl Grey' is short for 'Early'?

Heard at work

THAT MEETING PUT ME TO SLEEP.

Heard at Metropolitan and Bedford, Williamsburg

MY SHOWER IS MOODIER THAN MY EX.

Heard in the East Village

I GOTTA GET LADY-FIED.

Heard at Sweatshop, Williamsburg

WHO SAID
FOOD DELIVERY
BICYCLES WEREN'T
EMERGENCY VEHICLES?

Don't look now,
but Stanley Tucci
is behind you.

Heard in SoHo

Heard at All Saints in SoHo

YOU'RE YELLING AT ME WITH YOUR EYES!

Heard at work

I'M GONNA FOLLOW YOU TILL I GET WHAT I WANT...

Heard by my desk

I THINK I DID
BUT I DON'T
THINK I KNOW
I DID.

Heard by my desk

I'm sleep
deprived man,
I don't care.

Heard at Williamsburg Cinemas

FIFTY SHADES OF

Oh shit my mom's home!

Heard at Metropolitan and Bedford, Williamsburg

NO, NO I BELIEVE YOU...

I JUST DON'T GIVE A SHIT.

Heard in SoHo

HOW WEIRD
WOULD IT BE
IF BIRDS' KNEES
BENT FORWARD?

Heard in Caulfield, Melbourne

NO PHONES AT THE CHEESE TABLE!

my mom told me so.

Heard by my desk

I GOT STRESSED OUT,
SO I PUT ON A HELMET.

Heard by my desk

Heard at Metropolitan and Bedford, Williamsburg

YOU'RE THE
KIND OF GUY
WHO'D STOP
AT A
RED LIGHT
IN GTA.

IT'S SO HARD
NOT TO LISTEN
TO YOU!

Heard by my desk

Heard in the meeting room

EVERY TIME
YOU SAY 'PIZZA',
THIS SALAD
TASTES WORSE.

Heard at the gym

DOING WEIGHTS WITHOUT CARDIO IS LIKE OPENING THE HOOD OF A FERRARI AND FINDING TWO DUCKS IN THERE INSTEAD OF AN ENGINE.

Heard in the East Village

I need pizza or a nap...

haven't decided yet.

Heard at Sweatshop, Williamsburg

Heard by my desk

Do you wanna talk about it here or next to my potato?

Heard by my desk

Why are there no Dr Pepper Cocktails?

welcome to New York,

Where trash emerges from hibernation under those ambiguously grey piles of snow.

Heard at the gym

Heard in Broadmeadows, Melbourne

WHAT ARE YOU EATING?
WHY DON'T I HAVE ANY?

Heard on the corner of Hudson and Houston

I'LL STAND BY HIM BUT I WANNA CLUB HIM IN THE FACE

WHAT WOULD

KANYE DO?

Heard at work

Heard at work

HOW ARE YOU
NOT DEAD
OR ARRESTED?

Seen on my Facebook Newsfeed

The worst thing
about this weather
is the small talk
people try to make
about it.

Heard in Bed-Stuy

WHY YOU CRYING?
YOU'RE FIVE!
GET A JOB!

Heard at work

EVERYONE
ELSE
IS
STUPID.

Heard in a cab in Bed-Stuy

I JUST SNEEZED AND MY WHITE STRIPS FLEW OFF.

Heard by my desk

DON'T MAKE ME CRY WHILE I'M EATING A SANDWICH!

Heard by my desk

IF YOU HAVEN'T
CHANGED YOUR
NAME AT LEAST
ONCE IN YOUR LIFE,
YOU HAVEN'T

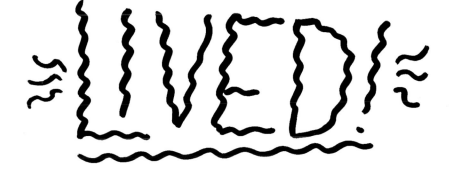

Heard at work

I AM A BOWL OF GUACAMOLE IN A WORLD OF FRESH AVOCADOS.

Heard by my desk

YOU SHOULD SEE INSIDE MY HEAD... IT'S LIKE A RAVE.

Follow
@_eavesdropper
On Instagram!

"Rick Padgett has done a phenomenal job of connecting the dots between prayer and every other area of the Christian life and walk. *Get Prayer* is a battle manual for the spiritual war for our souls."

BRANDON COX
Editor, www.Pastors.com
Editor, *Rick Warren's Ministry Toolbox*
Founding Pastor, *Grace Hills Church, Bentonville, Arkansas*

"Humorous, helpful and hope-generating, Rick Padgett unpacks prayer like a pro. Whether you are confused by the why, confounded by the when, or confronted by the who of prayer, Rick walks you through your resistance straight into the arms of a loving God. *Get Prayer!*"

MARNIE SWEDBERG
Author, Speaker, International Life Maximization Mentor
www.Marnie.com

"Don't let the title fool you. Rick Padgett's book, *Get Prayer and Get It All*, is not a simplistic pushbutton solution to a closer relationship with God. As a person who has studied prayer practically and theologically at the graduate level and experienced its power and effect personally, I can tell you Padgett is right on track. Prayer is about relationship and realizing the abundance of God's love! This book is a helpful and inspiration guide for those longing for a deeper and more powerful relationship with God—the lover of our souls."

LISA COLÓN DELAY
M.A. Spiritual Formation, Author of *Life As Prayer* and *Dog in the Gap: Brief Explorations in Canine Care-Taking and Human Flourishing*
www.LisaDelay.com

"Most Christians I know aren't satisfied with their prayer lives. Even seasoned believers wonder at times if their prayers rise above the ceiling. Author Rick D. Padgett gets it—and he has practical ideas to help us better pray God's heart. *Get Prayer and Get It All* is a refreshing journey into God's Word to learn the what and why of prayer, find examples of when and how to pray, and grow in communion with our Creator. Indeed, prayer is God's idea. He longs for us to know just how much He loves us—and to give us an opportunity to freely express our love for Him. Through rich biblical content and relevant personal stories—plus interactive online content to take you ever deeper—Padgett will help you plumb new depths of prayer and fathom all the more the all God has for you."

DEAN RIDINGS
Author, *The Pray! Prayer Journal (NavPress)*
Pray Every Day, www.facebook.com/prayerjournal

"In *Get Prayer and Get It All*, Rick Padgett writes a practical, powerful, interactive prayer journal directly from the heart of a loving Creator who desires an intimate, ongoing relationship with His Creation. Through his delightful story-telling and a rich history with God, Rick takes you on a journey through the scriptural foundations of prayer and models how to pray from a position of a favored son or daughter of the Almighty. He helps you understand that prayer is your direct access to the Throne of Grace, a sacred gift that connects your heart to His, and the only way to fully experience His presence, His power, and His promises. Though prayer, you will discover He is truly ALL you need."

MARY J. NELSON
Hosanna! Associate Pastor of Prayer
Author of *Grace for Each Hour, Hope for Tough Times,*
and *Peace for Each Hour*

"Rick Padgett has written a clear book on the complete power of prayer. *Get Prayer And Get It All* is a great guide to a deeper and more effective prayer life."

BOB MORTIMER
Founder, *Bob Mortimer Motivational Ministries*
Author, *Hope and Courage Across America*

"*Get Prayer and Get It All* is a new and refreshing perspective on a relational truth that has existed from the first day the first created man communed with his Creator. From the beginning, God purposed that we would live all of life from a continuous experience of All That He Is ...communing with All That We Are. In a world where prayer is perceived and lived as an intermittent part of our journey with God, a foray into a divine chamber in a time of need, want or brief worship, Rick Padgett defines a fresh picture of prayer as a continuous unbroken divine romance where both lovers give All to one another 'All the Time.'"

BOB NORSWORTHY
Executive Director
Newman Family Foundation

"A father's glowing love for his daughter prompts him to reflect on his heavenly Father's love for himself. Enlightening insights on stepping into God's presence and learning to trust Him completely. Loaded with valuable personal and practical applications. I learned a lot!"

RUSTY WRIGHT
International Lecturer
Author and Syndicated Columnist
www.RustyWright.com

"*Get Prayer and Get It All* encourages and motivates its readers to experience the joy of prayer. Instructions on prayer come only as a by-product to this journey. Brace yourself as you will not find a dry and boring prayer life here. As you follow the exercises at the end of each chapter, you just might find yourself on an exciting adventure with God."

KEVIN W. SHORTER
Author
www.Prayer-Coach.com

Get Prayer
and Get It All

Rick D. Padgett

GET PRAYER AND GET IT ALL

Publisher: Westgate Ministries, Portland, Oregon, www.RickDPadgett.com

Executive Editor: Ron Frey, Frey Resource Group, www.FreyResourceGroup.com

Managing Editor: David Sanford, www.LinkedIn.com/in/DRSanford

Editor: Naomi Inman, www.LinkedIn.com/in/NaomiInman

Designer: Anneli Anderson, www.DesignAnneli.com

This book comes in several convenient formats. The first is a free .pdf version you can forward via email to anyone you wish. The second is an inexpensive trade paperback edition available for sale on

- Amazon

- BarnesandNoble.com

- BooksaMillion.com

- ChristianBook.com

- www.CreateSpace.com/4468779

- other online book retailers

First Edition, October 2013

To Becky, my wife and fellow dreamer.

Thanks for believing when I needed it the most,

for seeing what no one else could see,

for helping me discover that dreaming

is not for the faint of heart.

Contents

Foreword

I'm often asked why I founded Hollywood Prayer Network, and why I think it's worth spending so much time trying to get people praying for Hollywood. My answer is because I believe, as Oswald Chambers did, that "Prayer does not fit us for the greater work; prayer is the greater work."

I am excited to be a part of any solid book about prayer, but *Get Prayer and Get It All* actually got me more excited about prayer than I've been for a long time. It rang true to three areas of passion for me that I think are very important to our faith: wanting ALL of God is the driving force of my faith; understanding my relationship with my FATHER in heaven and on earth is the key to our culture, our church, and my personal walk; and needing God desperately, and knowing that's right where He wants me, is my daily focus. Rick Padgett touched my heart with deep truths that we all need to know.

I particularly responded to *Get Prayer and Get It All* because—as I continue to learn more about prayer on my journey as a producer and a Christian in Hollywood—I appreciate books that go right to the core of the issue. If we are not completely sold out to God, if we don't need Him desperately, if we don't put Him above all else, then we are missing out on the abundant life that God promises us as His followers. And I believe the only way to experience that is through prayer.

I have lived through so many experiences I know I would not have gotten through without prayer. When our 22-year-old healthy, handsome, and talented son, Christopher, was 8 years old, he started having horrible headaches. They got so bad he could only lie down, and then he started vomiting. We brought him in to have a CT scan and we knew it was serious when his pediatrician came out from the testing room crying. She told us that he had a brain tumor in his head the size of an orange.

That day changed our whole life. Three days later, on Sunday, the day before major brain surgery, my husband, Jim, and I felt utterly spent. We had done all the needed preparations including choosing a doctor, a hospital, checking on our insurance, and committing to an approach we thought would be the best to beat this cancer. We turned to one another knowing we now were feeling the heavy weight of the circumstances and our son's impending life-or-death surgery.

At 11 a.m. that Sunday, even though our circumstances hadn't changed in any way, my husband and I suddenly both felt we had hope. Something lifted from us and we could feel more strength physically. We felt that way quite tangibly for the next two hours. By 1 p.m. we knew that, regardless of the outcome, God was faithful, He was in control, and we had to let go of our boy and trust him into God's hands.

The next day our 8-year-old son had surgery. Miraculously, the surgeon was able to remove the entire tumor. There were no side effects and, even better yet, no needed chemo or radiation. Four days later he left the hospital, missed only two weeks of third grade gym class, and after 10 years of clean MRIs, it was over!

A few days after Christopher's surgery, we learned that the previous Sunday—when my husband and I suddenly felt God had changed our hearts—a group of dear friends had gathered together from 11 a.m. to 1 p.m. to pray for us and for Christopher. Their two hours of prayer physically lifted us up and gave us the hope and strength to keep going. That experience changed me forever. When it comes to prayer, I am ALL IN, without a doubt, without wavering or hesitating. God has given ALL of Himself to us, so how can we do anything other than give our ALL to Him?

As you read this devotional, I urge you to embrace God's ALL. You may not know it yet, but all of us need Him desperately. Only then can He do miraculous works in our life—when we seek Him, depend on Him, and get out of the way. So, my prayer for you, as the reader of this book, is to turn to prayer and get God's ALL!

KAREN COVELL
Founding Director
Hollywood Prayer Network
www.hollywoodprayernetwork.org

1

GET PRAYER
AND GET IT ALL!

I choose a life of prayer because it is God's simple strategy to connect my life to His ALL.

On February 12, 1991, my private universe was completely deconstructed. The crisis began with the announcement we were expecting our first child. Like most first-time fathers, I had no idea what was hiding in my wife's womb. Silly me, I thought we were just having a baby. No one told me that a new master of my universe was about to appear. The nurse should have sounded the warning siren; instead she offered her standard announcement, "Congratulations, you have a daughter!" After twenty plus years, those words still hold their place as one of the single greatest *under*statements of all time.

The truth of the matter is I didn't *have* a daughter; instead, *she* had me. She invaded through my eyes and finger tips, going straight to the deepest places of my being, setting up her new government. Without thought or permission it happened in one refocusing blink. That wrinkly little bundle with a head full of wet ringlets, swirled in a mousse of amniotic fluid, threw down all opposition and assumed her supreme role as queen over my heart.

It would take a thousand stories to illustrate the power of my daughter's reign over me. One rather quirky result of our first encounter? For the first ten years of her life I couldn't bear the thought of cutting her hair. To me it violated the first thing I saw when we met. Her reign over me began with those reddish brown curls, and cutting them was like throwing her crown to the floor.

Another consequence of Caetlyn's invasion had to do with horses. Somewhere toward the end of our first decade together she developed a passion for all things equine. Her room became an equestrian shrine. Horse posters and hand-drawn pictures covered the walls, and horse figures and hats and riding boots lined shelf and hook and floor. Her longing led to riding lessons and eventually to the arrival of her royal charger. She named him "Dream Prince." The first time I saw them moving together, her royal hair rising and falling with his mane and tail, is permanently engraved on my heart.

I've never been a horse guy, but that didn't stop my heart from following her into this season of horses. Her longing became mine, her joy, my joy. *I was all in*. During the horse years that followed, I became the chief stable hand, performing many unsavory tasks: feeding the horse, catching the horse, picking out the horse's hooves, and even scooping recycled hay in service of the royal charger. I would do it all again for just one glimpse of the Queen and Dream Prince galloping in the afternoon sun, hair and mane rising and falling like a royal banner in the breeze.

I mention this to illustrate what I call the ALL moment, and to help you understand the title of this book, *Get Prayer and Get It All*.

As an 18-year-old young man, raised in poverty and broken circumstances, I encountered Jesus Christ and experienced the first overwhelming ALL moment of my life. My whole existence took on new meaning and purpose.

Years later as a new father, I experienced the ALL moment differently—*from the giving end*. This was a new definition, immediate, visceral, from the inside out. Although the word had been in my vocabulary, and the concept had been part of my theological training, now it was living in me every day. ALL was loose in my life.

That second experience planted an idea, a seed of understanding, deep into my soul about God and about prayer.

The ALL Exchange

What I discovered after the birth of my daughter was the moment when you can *joyfully* give yourself and everything you have to one person's welfare and never even blink at the "cost." In a singular ALL moment, my heart quickly and easily yielded total allegiance when confronted by something of absolute value. In my experience of ALL, courtesy of my daughter, I caught a glimpse how the deepest transactions of life are completed.

Without asking permission, the ALL moment of fatherhood activated a deep question of longing in my heart. Watching my heart respond to my daughter made me rethink God's Father love for me. I began to wonder in the deep places:

"Wow, God! Do you really feel this way about me?"

I began to suspect that ALL was much bigger than I thought. I was beginning to see that, if I followed this ALL beacon (lit by my daughter), it would redefine my faith, even changing my understanding of what it means to be human. I barely realized what had happened, yet found myself on a mission to experience the full and complete ALL exchange with God, my Father—to be loved in an undivided way, to reciprocate with undivided love. Deep rumblings were awakening in the hidden places of my heart.

While reading Genesis 1-2 through this lens, I came to the simple realization that on a particular day at the very start of human history, God became a Father. Have you ever considered that? God too had an ALL moment. He looked at His two children and named them and loved them without reserve. He told them, *"Everything I have is yours."* As a first-time Father, He experienced feelings of total devotion to His children on an epic scale.

Everywhere I looked this father-daughter journey pointed me into uncharted territory. I was being drawn into God's ALL, His uncalculating, undivided affection and commitment. I began to see why Jesus always emphasized the Father-child connection in how He prayed, and how He taught us to pray. **Prayer reconnects us with the Father's undivided, undiminished response to us. His response is always ALL.**

What if God can't wait to hear what I have to say, and can't wait to give to me from His ALL?

While trying to grasp the implications of God's undivided heart toward me, I recognized this simple connection: When a child needs a father's love or provision or special intervention, he or she simply *asks*.

As God's child, I too can ask my Father. I can count on my Father's undiminished, undivided resource to always be available for my life. He has put in place a simple strategy for me to access His love and provision and special intervention, and that strategy is prayer.

* * * * *

The Prayer That Became My New Best Friend: Ephesians 3:14-21

Although I had read the New Testament many times, *in the midst of my ALL discovery I found Ephesians 3:14 -21*. It became my new best friend. I found an uncanny match for what was going on in the deepest places of my heart. My questions and longings finally took shape as I traced my fingers over this prayer. Read it with me, and I think you will see what I mean.

^{14}*For this reason I kneel before the* **Father**, ^{15}*from whom his whole family in heaven and earth derives its name.*

^{16}*I pray that out of* **his glorious riches** *he may strengthen you with power through his* **Spirit** *in your inner being,* ^{17}*so that* **Christ** *may dwell in your hearts through faith. And I pray that you, being rooted and established* **in love**, ^{18}*may have power, together with* **ALL** *the saints, to grasp how* **wide and long and high and deep is the love of Christ**, ^{19}*and to know this love that surpasses knowledge—that you may be filled to the measure of* **ALL** *the fullness of God.*

^{20}*Now to him who is able to do* **immeasurably more** *than* **ALL** *we ask or imagine, according to his power that is at work within us,* ^{21}*to him be glory in the church and in Christ Jesus throughout* **ALL** *generations, forever and ever! Amen.*

A-L-L. That three-letter word is a big order. This prayer is like a grocery list of ALL, with every phrase pointing to God's commitment and resource for my life.

It starts with "Father" and immediately points us to His bank account of "glorious riches." That makes perfect sense to any father, since ALL gets expensive! It points us to the plural ALL of the Trinity; God is *ALL in*—the Father, the Son, and the Holy Spirit. It expands even further by joining ALL to His love— wide and long and high and deep! It is far-reaching, for "all the saints"; no one is left out. This prayer tells us ALL is *big*: beyond anything we could ask or imagine. It will take eternity to explore the whole of it. Finally, it shows that we too can give our ALL back to Him as "glory in the church."

While reading and praying this passage, important things began to happen.

First, I memorized these words by simple repetition in prayer. I couldn't help myself. These words were mine and fit like a pair of well-worn slippers. These verses became the "home page" of my heart. I found myself returning to them over and over.

Second, this prayer exposed my allegiance to the story of my past. I had a lot of reasons (and you do as well) to attempt a "smaller" definition of ALL. The circumstances of life had lowered my expectations, so I had to choose. Would I choose Ephesians 3 or my résumé?

I made that choice when I turned my eyes to the cross of Jesus—God's greatest demonstration of ALL. I boldly resolved to turn my back on my personal story of want, failure, and self-effort. In this critical moment Romans 8:32 reassured me: *He who did not spare His own Son, but gave Him up for us ALL—how will He not also, along with Him, graciously give us ALL things?*

I couldn't escape this divine interrogation, so I abandoned my résumé and gladly chose God's promise of ALL. It became a fundamental question of discipleship, a core decision that wasn't optional. Eventually, it's a choice each of us has to make.

Third, the final consequence of the prayer of Ephesians 3:14-21 was so obvious I barely noticed until it was nearly complete. I had become like a child so busy with his favorite candy that he fails to notice it has turned his tongue completely red. In my case it turned my entire conversation with God to the color of ALL. Prayer became an exercise in ALL.

It is remarkably simple. As I approach prayer, I habitually begin with my limited and divided perspective. I live in a world where every tick of the clock and every breath remind me that I live in a world of subtraction and division. Ephesians 3, my new best friend, took my hand and guided my prayers. It repositioned my heart, pointing more and more often toward God's undivided and ever-present ALL.

The Shortest ALL Prayer: "Yes"

The worst thing that could happen is to excuse yourself from the ALL experience. The little voice whispering, "That is a great story, but it's not for me," should get the mute button. ALL is waiting, closer than you think, and it simply begins by praying "Yes." This is the first ALL prayer, the first word of the ALL language.

The "Yes" prayer agrees with God that His ALL is the answer to my deepest longings. It says, "I am willing." I am willing to realign my present expectations with God's original intent, not my broken résumé. "Yes" is the ticket to the incredible experience of ALL.

Paul's extravagant prayer in Ephesians 3 is a "Yes" prayer. I find the Scriptures are full of "Yes" prayers filled with ALL language: words like *every, favor, forever, endless, always,* and **unfailing.** These words repeat and amplify the undivided nature of God's response to us.

Men of faith penned these words, stepping out of their mud puddles and into God's beautiful blue ocean. They may have felt inadequate to communicate it, but they are shouting, "Come on in, the water is fine!"

The combined effect of all these voices? I could never again define prayer as anything less than leaving my *ALL-NOT* world behind and stepping into the presence of the God who can never be less, more, or other than wholly Himself. He simply *cannot* be divided or diminished.

Prayer now means standing in the Lord's presence and letting my divided thoughts and emotions give way to His amazing, astounding completeness.

* * * * *

Why Do We Pray?

We are simply children reconnecting with our loving heavenly Father. The singular longing for God's ALL in the human heart directs each of us to pray. At the birth of my daughter I discovered there was an "ALL-longing" in the deepest places of my heart: to be loved in an undivided way, and to reciprocate with undivided love. God's ALL still pulls at the heart of every person who longs to leave behind his or her *ALL-NOT* existence.

In the brief chapters that follow you'll discover some strategies for prayer that I've developed through my ALL-colored lens. I've learned these strategies by praying both personally and corporately, but **ultimately it is always Jesus Christ who disciples me into the love of God.** Jesus, the ultimate ALL guy, has taken me on a wonderful journey out of my fractured back story and into personal *wholeness* and *integrity* in prayer.

You cannot believe how incredible it is to lift up your undivided childlike heart toward our indivisible God, who longs to hear what we have to say. Imagine the possibilities if "all the saints" start connecting to the undivided ALL of our Father, who stands ready to fund this journey out of His "glorious riches."

I invite you to approach God's ALL every time you pray. You have His undivided attention, His undiminished resources, and His unequalled power with you in the simple act of prayer.

When was the last time you sensed and experienced God's ALL in your own heart and life?

It is **God's ALL** that justifies writing yet another book on the subject and inviting another generation into a life of prayer.

Imagine if that happens in *your* life.

Let your journey begin!

* * * * *

A Scripture-based Interactive Prayer from Ephesians 3:14-21

Father, I bring my heart and life to You as a child who bears your name. I come to learn how to agree with Paul's prayer in Ephesians 3. I choose this prayer as Your will over against all the evidence of my circumstances. I invite Your strength and power through Your Spirit into my inner being. I aspire to be a home for Jesus Christ to dwell in, where He is completely at ease. I pray that the roots of my emotions would find nourishment in Your love so that I can grasp Your love for me and believe it. I pray for an increased emotional capacity so that I can be filled with Your ALL when I pray. Thank You for doing so much more than I can imagine. My imagination is so small, but with Your power I can experience ALL You have for me. As You empower me to receive your ALL I ask that You would show me how I am being empowered to give You my ALL. Amen.

Getting ALL In!

1. **Your story is as valuable to God as** your child's story would be to you. It is a powerful starting place for growing in prayer. Name one or two of the greatest ALL moments in your life so far. Can you go back and describe the emotions you felt at the time? List them or discuss them with a friend.

2. **Does recalling those feelings begin** to help you grasp God's emotions for you? How would you begin to pray differently if you believed you have God's undivided presence and power with you when you pray?

3. **Jesus told two very short twin parables** about ALL moments. Read the parable of the treasure and the parable of the pearl in Matthew 13:44-45. To what do the "treasure" and "the pearl of great price" refer? What did the man, or the merchant, give in exchange for them? What emotions accompanied each investment?

4. **Your heart is designed for ALL moments**—for giving all of yourself and all your resources to One with resolute purpose and great joy. As you've seen in Jesus' brief parables, reflect on how the emotion of joy accompanied the ALL moments in your past. How does joy differ from "happiness" and how does joy keep us motivated in hard times?

There's More!

Please visit RickDPadgett.com where you'll find interactive online content and bonus articles related to the chapters in *Get Prayer and Get It All*.

While you're online, I invite you to visit my Blog, Facebook page or Twitter feed.

- RickDPadgett.com/ricks-blog

- www.Facebook.com/RickDPadgett

- Twitter.com/RickDPadgett

I would love to hear from you:

- My email address, RickDPadgett@gmail.com

2

GET PRAYER AND GET
THE FIRST COMMANDMENT

*I choose a life of prayer because it is the only way
I can fulfill the Greatest Commandment to love
God and love people.*

Imagine being surrounded by a pack of legal experts looking to make a name for themselves. That's where you often find Jesus throughout the Gospels, and especially in Mark 12:18-31. These lawyers didn't specialize in just one arena of people's lives, such as constitutional or business or divorce attorneys do today. Instead, they meddled in every detail of everyone else's life. In essence, they functioned much like the elite Supreme Court clerks of Jesus' day, interpreting and arguing and ruling on every aspect of life using the Law of Moses and the writings about those laws handed down over the centuries. These are NOT the people who get invited to your backyard barbecue.

In Mark's Gospel we read about one of these lawyers who stepped forward to ask Jesus about the first or greatest or most important commandment. He had just heard Jesus giving the other lawyers *a good answer*. Maybe he was hoping to win a long-standing argument or prove a point, or maybe his question was sincere.

> *One of the teachers of the law came and heard them debating. Noticing that Jesus had given them a good answer, he asked him, "Of all the commandments, which is the most important?"*
>
> *"The most important one," answered Jesus, "is this: 'Hear, O Israel: The Lord our God, the Lord is one. Love the Lord your God with all your heart and with all your soul and with all your mind and with all your strength.' The second is this: 'Love your neighbor as yourself.' There is no commandment greater than these."*
>
> *"Well said, teacher," the man replied. "You are right in saying that God is one and there is no other but him. To love him with all your heart,*

*with **all** your understanding and with **all** your strength, and to love your neighbor as yourself is more important than **all** burnt offerings and sacrifices."*

When Jesus saw that he had answered wisely, he said to him, "You are not far from the kingdom of God." And from then on no one dared ask him any more questions.

The fact that Jesus spots one man in this pack of wolves and embraces him tells me that Jesus had just spotted a sincere man with a sincere heart. Jesus saw something in that one man that got his attention and that made him reach out and connect.

Like any lawyer this man wanted to win. I think Jesus wanted him to win as well, so he gave him a straight answer: "Love God with your all." I think he was telling the lawyer, "Give your ALL to the only One with the power to give His ALL to you. Then you will know how to love your neighbor." In the highest court of all, Jesus assured him, loving God first covers ALL the bases and it takes everything you've got. When those two happen, you win, others win.

In short, love always wins.

Jesus, being the ultimate ALL guy, wanted this one lawyer to win the only case that really matters. He wanted to see this man live a life that would hold up under the judgment of eternity. In speaking to a collection of lawyers, Jesus' answer left no loopholes: there were a whole lot of *alls* in this greatest commandment. Rest assured, when that one lawyer went away, he left knowing he had his answer. He knew love must come first. That's how we win.

The question is, do you want to win?

Do you want your life to demonstrate the greatest statement ever made about God's authority and desire? Then God's love must be the *first consideration* in all that we do, think, and feel. That is Jesus' formula for a wildly successful life.

You may be thinking, *That's a great platitude or ideal, but what does that look like? How do I explore this question of loving God and apply it to everyday life in practical ways?*

Jesus demonstrated how to do this. He practiced and exemplified what I like to call *the four common laws of love.* Let's explore how these common laws of love relate to prayer.

In the process, we will see that *a life of love,* in obedience to the First Commandment, is *a life of prayer.*

Practicing the Common Laws of Love

1. The Geography of Love

Those who love want to be with each other. Love scorns separation and distance, always straining to close the gap between lover and beloved.

One of the most beautiful statements ever made about the geography of love is found in the story of Ruth and Naomi. Ruth's vow of covenant love is built on geography, *"Where you go I will go, and where you stay I will stay. Your people will be my people and your God my God. Where you die I will die, and there I will be buried."* For Ruth, even separate gravesites drew a line of separation she would not endure. That is a profound commitment to the physical geography of love: nearness, closeness, touching.

We desire to share all of life's activities *with* those we love—whether it's sleeping, eating or work. **Being together is the gold standard by which lovers judge all things.** Anything that cooperates is a friend; conversely, anything that keeps lovers apart is an enemy. If you want a practical measure of your love relationships, ask yourself, *"How bothered am I by separation?"* Physical nearness is the first law of love.

Another example of God's commitment to nearness is in the name *Immanuel,* given to Jesus Christ by the prophet Isaiah 700 years before his birth (Isaiah 7:14, 8:8; Matthew 1:23). In Hebrew, *immanu-El* means the with-us-God. The hope of the ages took on the form of a human being to demolish the tragic separation in the Garden—to close the gap—because that is what love does.

Geography is the first law of love.

2. The Voice of Love

Those who love long to communicate. Love scorns silence. The only bigger contradiction to love than separation is silence. Even if lovers can't always close the geography gap, they long to communicate—to hear and be heard. Words are the sustaining sacrament of love.

Intimacy requires and demands a voice. There is no such thing as silent love. Even non-verbal communication between lovers is decoded and "heard." Lovers can't help themselves, always straining to hear the voice of the one they love, always desiring to keep the conversation going. We want to know, *What would my beloved say about that?* We once had letters and phone bills to prove that lovers must speak. Now we have instant gratification for those needing to hear and be heard. Texts, and emails and video calls are expressions of this law of love.

It is no accident that Jesus Christ is called "the Word" by "the disciple whom Jesus loved." The introduction to John's Gospel is a love shout. God broke the silence in the coming of His Son. Why? Because this is what lovers do. Want a great measure of your love relationships? How bothered are you by silence? Do you long to hear your beloved's voice? If so you are probably in love.

Communication is the second law of love.

3. The Vision of Love

Those who love have a singular vision and focus that allows them to see what others don't see. Love scorns distractions. When lovers are together they have the ability to block out distractions, even the legitimate demands of life, and fix their gaze and attention on the object of their love and delight. The clock disappears and "extra" friendships are shelved. Everything not directly connected to the lover fades into the gray periphery.

At the same time, a lover's gaze has a myopic focus that overlooks or excuses faults plainly obvious to others. With such intense focus you would think liabilities become more prominent, but love's vision is blind to such concerns.

I have done a limited amount of pre-marital counseling, but I have observed the "fixed gaze" of lovers is profound. When I divide a piece of paper into two columns and ask engaged couples to list their fiancé's or fiancée's assets on one side and liabilities on the other, invariably the liability side is short. They are blind to their lover's deficits.

Obviously, being "blinded by love" is not always helpful, but it does illustrate why Scripture makes such big deal about our eyes. Lovers know the power of a fixed gaze. If our eyes are in the right place, fixed on the right things, then usually all is well. If our eyes wander, then trouble is about to start.

The power of a fixed gaze is the third common law of love.

4. The Math of Love

Love doubles joy and divides sorrow. This miracle math defines the core delight of being in love. Love scorns apathy. Lovers want to know "What makes my beloved happy?" so they can multiply it, and "What makes my beloved sad?" so they can minimize it.

The lover finds it inconceivable that sorrow or joy would not be shared. They have learned to "weep with those who weep and rejoice with those who rejoice" (Romans 12:15). It's just what lovers do. Anything less is a contradiction of the primary mandate taught and demonstrated by Jesus. The math of doubled joy and divided sorrow is not optional. It is the fourth law of common love.

Those who love do many peculiar and mysterious things. However, these four universal behaviors form the baseline definition of intimacy—which is *love in action*. If we aspire to obey the command of Jesus to be lovers, this sort of practical definition moves us past platitudes and into real practice—what Jesus summarized in the greatest commandment. He didn't point to a hidden standard or a mysterious way of life. Instead, He challenged the lawyer (and, by extension, the rest of us) to be honest about what we already know.

Jesus' words and life force us to one simple and honest conclusion: Nothing is more important to God than a one-on-one loving relationship with you and me. We can experience that one-to-one intimacy only through a life of prayer *because prayer is about being with God*. Simple authentic prayer is about doing what lovers do best—being together.

Prayer is not a monologue. Instead, it's an exchange of voices. Prayer is a conversation that depends on a listening ear and an active expression. Prayer, like lovers and close friends, needs a place of undistracted meeting to center our focus on one another—us and God. We are all busy, but love still whispers, calling us to the secret place. Prayer is about both parties sharing their joy and sorrow. When these emotions arise, prayer is always near. Learn to stop and tell God about your enjoyment and your difficulties. Then draw up your courage and ask God to help you listen while He does the same. This is a simple and life-changing practice.

The conclusion? Jesus still offers us the same strategy He gave to the lawyer. He is showing us how to build a life that will hold up under the judgment of eternity, a life anchored by intimacy with God in the most common way of prayer. He knows what awaits at the end of our race and sets out a simple strategy for success: so simple that we can miss it, yet so challenging we will spend our lives trying to master it.

Remember, God wants us to win most of all. His plan is that the Final Victory will be an epic demonstration that love always wins.

* * * * *

A Scripture-based Interactive Prayer from Mark 12:29-31

Father, I come to surrender to the First and Greatest Commandment—the highest expression of Your authority and Your desire ever recorded in the language of men. I believe You are inviting me to the simplicity of being a common lover. With my eyes on Your Son I begin this journey of love by saying I am willing to learn what it means to be with You. I am also willing to learn how to hear and be heard in our relationship. I turn my back on anything that says, "Silence is acceptable." I also want to understand the mystery of our shared joy and sorrow. This seems so far away, yet it is how lovers act and think. I am willing to start again; thank You for being more than willing to start with me. I also know that I need to rediscover the power of a lover's eyes. I simply must see You as my lover, and I must experience the power of Your fixed gaze on me. It really is in the eyes of our beloved that we learn love, and I am here to learn. Thank You, Father, for the simplicity of Your Son's obedience. Thank You for the confidence that He is in me working that same simple obedience. I am excited for this renewal of our love relationship. Amen.

Getting ALL In!

1. **Look up and read Deuteronomy 6:4-9**, likely the best known passage of the Torah in Jesus' day, and also known in the Jewish tradition as the Great *Shema*. Which statements stand out to you? How do they relate to the Greatest Commandment?

2. **Which ways do you see the** "common law of lovers" reflected in Moses' practical instructions for families about loving God? Name the geography, content, and visual elements you find in this passage. Which elements seem most important to you?

3. **If you read past the "First Commandment" story, Mark 12:28-34, you soon bump into the story of the widow's two coins, Mark 12:41-44.** Do you think this is coincidental or intentional? What does this story tell us about the message of ALL? Was the widow a "common lover"? How does this story compare with the Mark 14:1-9 story of the woman who poured perfume on the feet of Jesus?

3

GET PRAYER AND
GET THE SON

*I choose a life of prayer because I see no other
way to receive ALL that Jesus purchased for me
and to give Him ALL that He deserves.*

Sports were the glue of my pre-adolescent world. I probably got infected
with the love of games from my older brother, but athletics really became
central when I enrolled in public school. Competition became a way of life.
Waiting for the bus in the morning involved street football. Gym classes promised indoor games, and when the recess bell rang I bolted for outdoor games
of anything with a ball. Most of us put off going home after school to resume
play in an empty lot. Our seasons were marked by the shape and size of the
ball we threw, caught, batted, and kicked.

I made friends in this world of competition and a few enemies too. Looking
back I cannot remember one friendship during my early years that had not
sprouted from the soil of a ball-field. We played ball at every opportunity, so
having a friend outside our athletic endeavors seemed pointless at best.

The dreaded "team picking" was a daily tribal ritual. The best athletes became
team captains and took turns choosing players based on skill and allegiance.
Players without skill or allegiance were ruthlessly ignored until they were
placed on a team by default. You did not want to be one of those kids.

My best friend was a poster child for how to survive in this world of boy-
hood games. Bruce had skill and that made allegiance easy. He also had a fierce
competitive streak to boot. We never discovered a game he couldn't master.
Not only did he master the big three—football, basketball, baseball—but he
went on to build an impressive array of success in other sports. Tennis, track,
racquetball, bowling, handball, and even Ping-Pong yielded to his innate speed
and coordination.

Our high school PE instructor was a former Olympic athlete. He took on my
friend, Bruce, in a handball match. Bad idea. It was not a good day for Coach

Gus; Bruce dominated the match. We all watched in disbelief as Coach Gus finally resorted to cheating, including calling several game-winning shots "out-of-bounds." Although Coach eventually "won" the match, Bruce won our enduring respect. His fame only increased.

If the legend of my friend ended here, it would be a nice enough story, but I left out one important fact. Bruce had only one arm. All his athletic accomplishments were literally done single-handedly. He lost the use of his right arm and shoulder at birth, courtesy of forceps in the hands of an over-zealous country doctor. By the time his parents realized that his arm and shoulder were not developing, the damage to his nerves and ligaments was permanent. His right arm would remain shriveled and twisted for the rest of his life.

Bruce's friends soon learned to ignore his handicap. To be his friend, it's likely that you had been the unwary opponent of a one-armed game. To say his talent disarmed the uninitiated, well, that was just too tempting! Every time an unfamiliar player let his guard down due to Bruce's disability, he was in for a good dose of humiliation. It was great fun to watch. I saw scores of boys join the Coach Gus club.

Bruce once hit three home runs in a single softball game because the right fielder refused to play deep for a one-armed batter. Bruce rightly earned the title of the One-Armed Bandit. His friends and fans always said Bruce had an unfair advantage due to the misplaced compassion or naiveté of his competitors.

What they didn't know is Bruce's secret. He knew he could never win by playing to the way others saw him. He assumed his identity as an athlete and refused to accept an identity as a handicapped or disabled student.

I tell Bruce's story to illustrate a key principle of human experience, namely that every real success story must include more than just the facts of **what** was accomplished. Success cannot have a meaningful definition without including **how** it was accomplished. Often, as in the case of Bruce, it's the **how** that defines the story.

* * * * *

We're about to consider the greatest man of prayer who has ever lived. His batting average was 1.000. His prayers raised the dead, healed the sick, changed the weather, multiplied groceries, opened the heavens, called out demons, and directed angels. His prayers were so dynamic that His disciples asked, "Teach us to pray."

Everyone knows Jesus had a résumé of wildly successful prayers, but what many of us have never stopped to notice, however, is that behind these prayers was a much bigger story—the story of *how* He prayed.

* * * * *

Three Ways Jesus Prayed

When you get prayer, you get God's ALL in the form of His Son, Jesus Christ, the man who prayed like no other. However, it's important to remember that when Jesus prayed, He prayed as a man, showing us how to pray as men and women. In the words Jesus used, in the posture He assumed, He invited every believer to pray in their new identity.

We will consider what I call three *identity windows* of prayer: (1) as a royal son to our Abba Father, (2) as a beloved bride with love and anticipation, and (3) as a royal priest with total access to God's throne room.

These windows of (1) inheritance, (2) intimacy, and (3) access are unlocked through the offering of Jesus' life, His ALL, on the cross at Calvary for each and every believer.

The more I explore these windows of identity, the more I'm convinced that the practical pursuit of being a disciple of Jesus' is inseparable from the life of prayer.

1. Abba, Father: The Window of Inheritance

Jesus Christ always defined prayer as a child spending time with his Father.

> *This, then, is how you should pray: "Our Father in heaven..."* (Matthew 6:9).

If you were allowed to stand with Jesus in His most intimate moment, in the epic crisis of His life, you can hear Him redraw the boundaries for prayer with a single word. Abba.

> *"Abba, Father,"* he said, *"everything is possible for you. Take this cup from me. Yet not what I will, but what you will"* (Mark 14:36).

In one word, "Abba," Jesus lands in new territory for His generation. It's the territory of a loving Father-child relationship and all that implies. Through prayer Jesus appeals to His Father, the King, for His inheritance in the Kingdom. He prays as a royal Son. In this prayer He is inviting you and me to pray as a royal son, a royal daughter.

> *Because you are his sons, God has sent forth the Spirit of his Son into your hearts, crying out, "Abba, Father!" (Galatians 4:6; cf. Romans 8:15).*

No wonder Jesus goes straight for this place. He knew if prayer were a place where a son or daughter could approach a loving Father, then nothing could keep us from praying. He knew when this identity grips us, we will pray like He prayed. *He knew prayer was not a changeable behavior, but an expression of our unchanging identity as sons and daughters.*

Everything Jesus modeled and taught His disciples about prayer was leveraged on placing this deep reality in their hearts. We are sons and daughters appealing to an affectionate and loving Father who gives us His undivided attention and the undiminished resources of His kingdom.

Jesus brings us to prayer because He is the Son showing us how to be sons and daughters. He shows that the deep longings of the human heart connect with the deep longings of the Father's heart. He brings the longing and the language together to redefine prayer in a single word, *Abba.*[1]

2. Groom and Bride: The Window of Intimacy

Jesus Christ opens another "identity" window to the life of prayer by inviting us into the story of the Groom and His Bride.

> [18]*Now John's disciples and the Pharisees were fasting. Some people came and asked Jesus, "How is it that John's disciples and the disciples of the Pharisees are fasting, but yours are not?"*
>
> [19]*Jesus answered, "How can the guests of the bridegroom fast while he is with them? They cannot, so long as they have him with them. [20]But the time will come when the bridegroom will be taken from them, and on that day they will fast" (Mark 2:18-20).*

The story of the Groom and Bride overflows with pictures and impressions that stir both passion and emotions: courtship, betrothal, and marriage. Jesus' response to the people's confusion about fasting was radical. In plain sight, He announced Himself as the Bridegroom.

---

1 The strategic importance of this window will be discussed further in Chapter 4.

In the center of this story line Jesus placed a new definition of prayer. His disciples would no longer define prayer and fasting as a sacrificial response to difficult circumstances or personal failure. Instead, His disciples would now define prayer and fasting as the Bride's response in a prolonged engagement. Prayer becomes a lover's conversation, anticipating the final appearing of the Groom. It's no wonder the final prayer of Scripture is a one-word prayer of agreement between the Spirit and the Bride: "Come!"

Just as desire reaches an apex during engagement and immediately before the wedding, Jesus awakens desire in the heart of every believer by choosing us as His Bride. Jesus used the bridal language to describe the gap between the first and second coming. In doing so, He transformed the discussion from a theological debate into the greatest romance in human history.

If you embrace the story of Jesus as your Bridegroom, and you as His Bride, you will soon be asking yourself, "Does the Son really want to be that intimate with me?"

In the same way that "Abba" opens our heart to intimacy with the Father, learning to call Jesus our Bridegroom opens our heart to intimacy with the Son. The conversation of longing between the Church and her Bridegroom is for every believer. It is essential to our growth as disciples and it is critical to God's strategic plan to sustain our hearts. Your opportunity to explore this treasure starts right now and lasts until the wedding day arrives. Have you told your Bridegroom how you feel about Him lately?

3. Priest: The Window of Access

The final way Jesus Christ radically redefines the life of prayer is by opening the priesthood to include all believers.[2] As a believer in Christ, there is nothing between us and God when we pray. Nothing.

Jesus' final offering of His life to God was a perfect sacrifice, forever eliminating the need for an *intermediary* between us and the Father when we pray. The cross of Jesus Christ was the ultimate ALL event when the earth shook and the Temple curtain ripped open to let us in. It was an unbelievable event for the ancient Jewish people, who had known only formality and separation from God's room, the Holy of Holies.

This passage from Hebrews 4 is a real confidence builder.

---

2 This window of access, like the previous two, is so profound that it's impossible to contain in a few short paragraphs. It's my hope that you will further explore the wonder of your priestly status in our online resources at www.RickDPadgett.com.

> *[14]Therefore, since we have a great high priest who has ascended into heaven, Jesus the Son of God, let us hold firmly to the faith we profess. [15]For we do not have a high priest who is unable to empathize with our weaknesses, but we have one who has been tempted in every way, just as we are —yet he did not sin. [16]Let us then approach God's throne of grace with confidence, so that we may receive mercy and find grace to help us in our time of need (Hebrews 4:14-16).*

Jesus' life offered the perfect sacrifice by the perfect man to cover once and for ALL the sins and *reproach* of everyone who believes. We are made *complete* or *perfect* in Jesus Christ, able to *approach* God's throne with confidence. That, my friend, is access: access to God's ALL!

Your prayer may be stumbling, you may feel your prayer imperfect, but *in Jesus Christ* your prayers and intercession are completely *acceptable* to God. Peter reminds us that, when you are *in Jesus Christ*, and when you pray, you are a priest offering a spiritual sacrifice.

> *You also, like living stones, are being built into a spiritual house to be a holy priesthood, offering spiritual sacrifices acceptable to God through Jesus Christ (1 Peter 2:5).*

Have you ever thought of praise and prayer as your *primary* "priestly" duty? Do you really believe the throne room is always open to you? Have you considered how much God treasures *every* time you pray?

In Revelation you'll find a moving word picture about *the treasure of our prayers*. When the four living creatures and the twenty-four elders kneel before the Lamb in heaven's throne room, they hold "golden bowls full of incense, which are the prayers of God's people" (Revelation 5:8, 8:3). Every time you pray, you are making a deposit or investment into one of these golden bowls.

Every time a believer prays, he or she is ministering with Jesus in the heavenly throne room. Prayer is standing with Jesus in the midst of the angels and the living creatures, partnering with Him, and contending for the joining of heaven and earth.

I find it hard to imagine a greater access to God's ALL than entering His throne room. Yet this rite of priesthood, this spiritual sacrifice, happens only *when we pray.*

Our priestly identity is the final "identity window" given to every believer in Jesus Christ.

The three *identities* we "get" in God's Son, Jesus Christ, can forever revolutionize our prayers. As (1) God's sons and daughters, (2) as the Bride of Jesus Christ, and (3) as priests with Christ, our confidence in prayer can grow and grow.

The longer we meditate on the life of Jesus, the more our ministry of prayer will grow and expand. After all, when we get the Son, we get prayer *and* God's ALL!

* * * * *

A Scripture-based Interactive Prayer from Hebrews 4:14-16

Abba Father, I stand with Your Son, Jesus Christ, my High Priest. I fix my eyes on Him, the one who opened the way for me to approach Your throne with confidence. I am here to learn of the priestly ministry, to do what He is doing. Help me to understand how to partner with Him in the ministry of prayer, my offering of incense to You. I want to experience all that was purchased for me on the Cross, the ultimate sacrifice made by the greatest High Priest. Open my understanding and my emotions to this ministry so that I might make a right offering of my life and my heart. Amen.

Getting ALL In!

The secret behind the prayers of Jesus is His identity, the same identity He shares with us. Identity cements the things that will always be true of our relationship with God. There will never be a time when we will cease to be sons or daughters, priests, or the Bride of Jesus Christ. When we learn to pray this way, we are praying in a direct link with eternity.

1. **Read Galatians 4:6-7,** part of which was quoted above. What is the opposite of God's child? What rights does the opposite have? In contrast, what rights do you enjoy?

2. **Read John 3:29.** How did John the Baptist refer to Jesus and what emotion did he feel when he said it? Now read Mark 2:18-20 (see also Matthew 9:14-15 and Luke 5:33-35). How did Jesus refer to Himself and what are some practical ways we can we train our emotions to fit His description?

3. **Read 1 Peter 2:4-5, 9.** As priests, what are our spiritual sacrifices? What makes them acceptable to God? To what degree has this been your experience so far? Can you imagine praying differently from here on out?

4

GET PRAYER AND
GET THE FATHER

*I choose the life of prayer because it is the only
way to experience life as a child of my Father.*

My friend Cliff has traveled with me on this journey toward being a lover of
God. For three decades now, Cliff has traveled both the roads and the crossroads of life with me. As a friend and a mentor, he's been there for me through
almost all of the big decisions and events that have shaped my life. More than
any other person, he's helped me define my life aspiration to love God and be
a man of prayer.

Yet, as someone who has helped so many others, his earthly journey is the
exact opposite of what you might think if you were to meet him today.

As a child Cliff watched his family torn by alcoholism and mental disease.
His biological father sired six children but never knew how to be a dad. He
poisoned their lives with poverty, fear, violence, abuse, and constant shame.
While Cliff's father lived at the tavern, Cliff's mother lived in her bed. She was
mentally ill, chronically depressed, and almost never left her room. She left the
care of the house to little Cliff and his oldest sister. She was eventually committed to a mental care facility, a place from which she would never return.

The big trouble started when his father's criminal activity landed him in pris-
on, again. Now Dad was totally gone, mom was in bed, and six children were
left to fend for themselves. It took six months before authorities discovered the
family's appalling plight: six children living in utter squalor, lice infected and
hungry. Cliff tells this part of the story: "It must have been pretty bad because
they started a fire and burned our clothes and personal belongings. The only
thing we were allowed to keep was a small collection of family photos."

In one life-altering afternoon, a government worker bundled up six children
and packed them into a government vehicle. They sent them to the State Home
for Orphans, hundreds of miles away. Authorities promised not to separate the
family, but that promise disappeared as they buckled under the difficulty of

placing six children in a single home. They opted to send 9-year-old Cliff and his older sister to one home while four younger siblings were sent to another.

You can easily imagine Cliff's heart became a dungeon of bitterness and anger, built with thick walls of disappointment and betrayal. To amplify this cruelty, the first family to adopt him didn't stick. They sent him back with a laundry list of Cliff's "incompatibilities." He was "too broken, too un-relational." So Cliff and his sister went back into state custody, each passing month pushing them further past the ideal age for adoption. As the months turned to years, no one could have guessed that Cliff's story was about to take a dramatic turn.

The Wendell family was the U-turn marker in Cliff's journey. After the tragic death of their own daughter, they considered adoption. As they began to explore the possibility of opening their hearts to a child who needed a home, they heard about Cliff and his sister. I am sure they debated whether they were ready for two new additions to their family, and they also had a surviving son who would have to sign off on the adventure. But whatever the process, they finally decided to go ahead with the adoption. Cliff was twelve years old when he was introduced to his "third" family. The fear of rejection hung heavily on his heart. He probably thought, *"I'll be rejected again."*

About two weeks after Cliff and his sister arrived at their new home, the family attended a large gathering of extended relations and friends. As the crowd filled the meeting place and people broke into smaller conversational groups, Cliff's new dad did something that forever changed his life. Without warning or even asking permission, he put his arm around Cliff and began to take him around the room, stopping at each group, and saying "Have you met *my son*, Cliff?" He would then go through the exchange of names and move to the next group. This was a large gathering and the process was repeated in at least ten separate groups.

Somewhere around the fourth time Mr. Wendell introduced Cliff as "my son," Cliff's heart changed. He knew this man was actually telling the truth. Even though Mr. Wendell had another son, there was plenty of room in this man's heart for Cliff to be "my son."

Light suddenly streamed into Cliff's dungeon of anger and disappointment. By the time they had toured the room, two single-syllable words, "my son," had blown the dungeon door off its hinges, and Cliff followed his "real dad" out of that darkness forever.

Though he didn't have the words yet, Cliff knew this man had taken complete ownership of his young heart and life. Cliff finally had a place of belonging. His identity as a son was a dramatic revelation. From that time on, to hear Cliff tell the story, he followed his new dad like a puppy. "Whatever he did, I did. Wherever he went, I went," Cliff said. "I couldn't get enough of that guy!"

To this day Cliff's adoptive father is the hero of Cliff's heart. Their father-son stories are a treasury. Mr. Wendell received Cliff and spoke over him one repeated and powerful affirmation, "my son," breaking twelve years of silence, disappointment, rejection, and pain.

Although Cliff's journey is not one any of us would choose, all of us long to experience what Cliff discovered, a place of *belonging* and *identity*.

It is no coincidence that the public ministry of Jesus was framed with these same two words—"My Son" (Luke 3:22; see also Matthew 17:5).

So, what is the hidden superpower behind these two words?

Their power lies in the fact that when the Father spoke them over Jesus, *He was not simply targeting one heart, but rather the whole human race, all of us who collectively long for a place of belonging and identity, resource and security*.

It is my hope that this chapter will help you discover that God intends for each of us to experience the power of the Father's voice that so radically altered Cliff's life.

* * * * *

The Baptism of Jesus

When Jesus Christ emerged from the waters of baptism, we hear the greatest statement in all of human history. It is the phenomenal claim of *The* Father over *The* Son.

> *When all the people were being baptized, Jesus was baptized too. And as He was praying, heaven was opened and the Holy Spirit descended on Him in bodily form like a dove and a voice came from heaven, "You are my Son, whom I love; with you I am well pleased" (Luke 3:21-22, see also Matthew 3:13 and Mark 1:9).*

When I first understood the significance of the Father's voice in Luke 3, I realized the Father's voice reverberates to every one of His children. In my heart I could hear my Father telling me, "You, Rick, are My son." How I longed to hear that again and again.

Part of my eagerness was that, like Cliff, I had a huge deficit in the "father department." I came into the faith as a broken boy without a father. My father died suddenly when I was seven, and my world crumbled. My longing for a father's voice was met by years of silence.

Maybe that's why I so identify with Cliff's story. Maybe it's why I can see so clearly the radical nature of what happened on the shores of the Jordan. When I heard these words, "my son," I knew there was room for me in the ALL of the Father's love.

The Father's words to Jesus—"You are my son, whom I love; with you I am well pleased"— touch the life of each person who is in Jesus Christ, from the time of Jesus Christ until now. If only we knew it!

The power of the Father's affirmation released in these verses explains everything else that happens in Jesus' public life and ministry. Remember, they were spoken on the occasion of Jesus' public debut.

The baptism of Jesus is a picture that rewards our careful attention by revealing details a casual observer may not observe. So, I will deliberately slow the frames of this event. That way, you and I can get a good look at what is happening.

The Trinity

One detail that is easy to notice is an unprecedented appearance by all three members of the Trinity. Nowhere else in the Scriptures do we so clearly see all three persons of the Trinity interrupt human history at the same moment. Talk about an ALL event! If this were the only thing you knew about this story, it should be adequate cause to give these words our careful consideration.

John the Baptist

The scene opens as Jesus enters the waters of the Jordan River, a mere creek by my Pacific Northwest reckoning. In so doing, Jesus associates Himself publicly with his trouble-causing cousin. The two men know each other, but it is hardly a cozy cousin friendship. John's entire life has been an assault on human and societal protocol. He is a human battering ram of epic proportions.

Jesus not only associates Himself with John, but is just about to take John's lifelong work to new heights. In fact, Jesus will soon steal John's favorite one-line sermon and use it to define his early ministry: "Repent, for the Kingdom of Heaven is at hand!"

Still, John is having trouble connecting the dots. As the two men talk, the discussion ends with John acquiescing to his cousin's request to be baptized. As soon as he does, the entire event shifts into a completely different category of human experience.

The heavens open!

The ancient Jewish people had a special category in their theology for mega events. By their standard they would put this moment on par with Moses encountering God on Mount Sinai. This was a 9.5 on their spiritual Richter scale! In order to read these words correctly, you have to remember the original audience. They wore ancient Hebrew reading glasses. They clearly knew that when the heavens part and things begin to come out of heaven to earth, you pay attention!

Now let's take a look at the words themselves. I think it is helpful to break them into three distinct statements, plus a bonus phrase hiding just beyond the crowd's hearing.

"You are My Son"

We encounter two compelling ideas in this phrase.

The first is *belonging*.

God's claim on our life is like a two-sided coin, one side declaring God's legal ownership and the other side activating a deep sense of emotional belonging.

Whenever God says, "Mine," big things happen. When God spoke this word over the ancient Israelites in Egypt, it set in motion the entire Exodus narrative.

The results are just as dramatic when God says "Mine" in the secret places of the human heart. When we experience it on a heart level, it feels like God is posting a huge "No Trespassing" sign on our lives. It puts all inappropriate claims on short notice; it is the beginning of true freedom.

"You are My Son" also sets in motion the second compelling idea, *identity*.

Putting these four words together, "You are My Son," activates one of the deepest laws of human existence, namely, that *identity always follows belonging*. They are inseparable. In the same way that God's "Mine" evicts all false claims on our lives, it also serves notice to all the false identities associated with those claims.

In the first Exodus, God's "Mine" transformed slaves into a chosen nation. At the baptism of Jesus Christ, it opens the way for orphans and prodigals to return the Father's house as sons and daughters. Do you see why I think these words should be in special high definition font? I hope so!

"whom I love"

The next three words multiply the first phrase. Again, this is *heart language*. The intimacy expressed in these words shows up in the Greek translation, "You are My Son, My Beloved." The Father is saying something that might strike us as obvious. Then again, lovers speak these words at every opportunity. The redundancy of the Father's love for Jesus awakens a desire in the heart of every witness for the same experience of extravagant love. Hearing the Father's voice was never meant to be a one-time event.

If we see this event and hear these words correctly, our feet involuntarily start to edge toward what is happening. The direct link between these words and the human heart literally begins to pull you toward Jesus. You might not be in the water yet, but I doubt you will be dry for long. The next phrase will practically pick you up and toss you into the water.

"with You I am well pleased"

This phrase further multiplies the power of everything that precedes it. If we just skim over the words, we might say it's obvious that the Father is pleased with Jesus. Yet if we feel our hearts respond to these words, something entirely different happens.

Our hearts crave this experience. Few things in life are more gratifying than the affirmation that comes from bringing enjoyment to someone we love. This dynamic is behind the giving of gifts. It's why we enjoy doing special favors, cooking favorite meals; mutual enjoyment is even at the core of God's design for marital sexuality.

If you doubt the power of this experience, simply ask yourself, *"What happens when my gifts of love are not received or go unnoticed? What happens when they're bypassed or rejected out of hand?"*

In these thirteen words, God the Son and God the Father are doing heart business on a large scale. You witness the progression of ownership, identity, affection, and affirmation in a class by themselves. Never has so much been said, so simply, for the good of so many.

Remember the Witnesses!

It seems important to pause and underline a key point in the story. This is not an embarrassing public display of affection that makes the onlookers uncomfortable. Instead, it is more like God inviting all of us to join the celebration.

The more you review this event, frame by frame, the more you see the big picture: that Jesus' baptism defined everything Jesus was about to reveal in His public ministry. In turn, that means it is for *all of us.*

In essence, this is a demonstration and an invitation to experience God's ALL in His ownership over your life and mine.

The Witnesses Watch the Fulfillment of Psalm 2

Some phrases in our culture pop out at us. Likewise, hundreds of years of shared cultural or religious literacy can make a few short words carry a world of meaning. When a crowd of Jewish witnesses saw Jesus come up out of the water, they saw the heavens parting and heard a very familiar phrase, *"You are My Son."*

I wonder if a holy hush may have stilled the crowd even further, their minds racing to the second Messianic Psalm. They knew how to complete the phrase. After all, they've heard it all their lives, and now I picture them wondering—almost in disbelief—*Is this really happening?*

The passage they would have remembered is recorded in Psalm 2:7-8.

> *⁷He said to Me,*
>
> *"You are My Son;*
>
> *Today I have become Your Father.*
>
> *⁸Ask Me,*
>
> *And I will make the nations Your inheritance,*
>
> *The ends of the earth Your possession."*

Almost any ancient Jewish witness could complete the phrase that came after *"You are My Son."* Likewise, each would know the rest of the story: that David's foreshadowed Messiah would inherit the earth and break the nations with a rod of iron, and bless all who take refuge in Him (Psalm 2:7-12).

Here, on this day, every one of their senses confirmed the longing of the ages before them. They could see and touch the man. They could hear the Father's voice declaring ownership of *His Son*. The familiar prophetic language rang loud and clear.

Psalm 2 was absolutely clear that the Messianic kingdom would be set in motion by the Father's declaration over His Son. The crowds on that shore had just been introduced to *God's Son*. They knew that the man standing in the Jordan had an *inheritance*. The ultimate Son steps out onto the stage of human history and lays claim to the ultimate throne, the throne that will rejoin heaven and earth.

Here was the Father, publicly declaring that Jesus is His delightful and dearly loved Son. The kingdoms of the earth would be His inheritance, His possession. Just when they might be wondering if John the Baptist was the One, that idea evaporated. Here He stood, the humble carpenter from Nazareth, yet so much more!

Most of us don't have a super-rich dad who can't wait to resource our dreams, yet all of us will admit that it is a very appealing option. Jesus was born with the ultimate silver spoon in His mouth, and the allusion to Psalm 2 in the Father's announcement makes that crystal clear.

The Devil Lurks

We cannot appreciate the whole story until we realize the audience included someone who was no friend. The unwanted eavesdropper had a better handle on the Scriptures than most of us. This particular Scripture was anything but music to that terrible enemy. Hearing those words must have enraged him.

What did this intruder hear? I believe he heard the Father restoring to Jesus what Adam had lost. Jesus came as the second Adam to fulfill the Father's original plan—that men and women, made in His image, would reign with Him on the earth. Jesus was ushering in a *new kingdom*. The new kingdom was His inheritance as God's sinless, spotless, perfect Son.

In the wilderness confrontation that followed, the Devil made a full frontal assault on Jesus' *identity* as God's Son, and on Jesus' *inheritance* of the kingdoms of the earth.

> *Jesus, full of the Holy Spirit, left the Jordan and was led by the Spirit into the wilderness, where for forty days he was tempted by the devil... The devil said to him, "If you are the Son of God, tell this stone to become bread."*

*The devil led him up to a high place and **showed him in an instant all the kingdoms of the world. And he said to him... "If you worship me, it will all be yours."***

"If you are the Son of God," he said, "throw yourself down from here..." (Luke 4:1-13).

In all three attacks, the Devil questioned Jesus' identity and inheritance as God's Son. We also can see that he inserted an "if" before God's "Mine," questioning everything the Father's voice had just declared to be true!

Of course, Jesus knew exactly what God had said and reminded His opposition by saying, "Man shall not live by bread alone, but by every word that proceeds from the mouth of God." I believe Jesus' response to the Devil may have included a little jab—a direct reminder to the enemy of the words the Father had just spoken at His baptism.

Considering the wilderness confrontation that followed Jesus' baptism, it is certain the Devil heard Jesus praying as He came up out of the water. Jesus' baptism prayer very well may have been a prayer of obedience straight out of Psalm 2:8, *"Ask of Me and I make the nations your inheritance."*

When the enemy offers Jesus a shortcut to possessing the nations, what does the Devil say? "Fall down and worship me and I will give you all..." Of course, this is an *imitation ALL* and Jesus doesn't take the bait. The Devil's claim that Jesus can possess His God-given inheritance apart from His Father parallels Genesis 3, where the serpent offers Eve the knowledge of good and evil apart from her relationship with God.

The more you reflect on the details of Jesus' baptism, the more you can understand how it frames His whole life and ministry, and our inheritance *with Him* as believers. The Father's voice dramatically introduces Jesus, unveiling His purposes for all to see.

In that moment we can discover the blueprint for how our own hearts respond to the Father's voice, and also how the Enemy targets our *identity* and *interaction* with the Father in order to sabotage our *inheritance*—or God's ALL for us.

It seems almost impossible to overstate the importance of this mega-event in a small collection of words.

Four ALLs of God

Before we move on to the interactive prayer and ideas for discussing this chapter, let's summarize the key points. First, the baptism was a unique visitation by all members of the Trinity. This brief thirteen-word description reveals four strategic truths that make up God's ALL—His undivided and undiminished promise to us. The four truths are:

The ALL of the Father's ownership (releasing identity and belonging)

The ALL of the Father's love

The ALL of the Father's enjoyment

The ALL of the Father's inheritance

In the center of this event Jesus is in the posture of prayer, pointing us once again to the main thesis of our study, that prayer is God's simple strategy for connecting our lives to His ALL.

I invite you to imagine yourself getting in the water with Jesus and receiving the Father's voice of ownership over you. Much as my friend, Cliff, would tell you, the Father's pronouncement establishes your identity and opens up a relationship that forever changes your destiny.

* * * * *

A Scripture-based Interactive Prayer from Luke 3:21-22

I come to you in prayer, Father, picturing John the Baptist and Jesus standing in the Jordan River. As Jesus prays, I see the Holy Spirit come out of heaven to Him. And I hear You say, "You are My Son." How I long to hear Your voice speaking those same words to me. Thank You for speaking them again and again on the pages of Scripture, and on the pages of my heart. Thank You for adopting me as Your own son/daughter. I'm forever grateful. I pray this in the wonderful name of Your Son, Jesus Christ, Amen.

Getting ALL In!

The follow-up for this chapter may be the most important section of this entire book. The focus of the baptism event is the restoration of God's original intent that He would co-reign on the earth with men and women made in His image and likeness. With that in mind, consider the following questions.

1. **Go to Genesis 1:24-28** and reread God's original plan for this shared reign. When God speaks in the plural saying, "Let *Us* make man in *Our* image," in what ways is this similar to or different from the Trinity showing up at the baptism of Jesus?

2. **Go to Numbers 6:22-27.** Which elements of the three baptism phrases from Luke 3 are in this priestly blessing over the Israelites? Now read verse 27 twice. Whose name is "put" or placed on the Israelites? What action does God take in response to His name (ownership) being placed the Israelites?[3]

3. **Read Ephesians 1:3-14.** What does this passage say to you about "getting in the Jordan with Jesus"? Be sure to re-read Ephesians 1:13b-14. What elements of Jesus' baptism do you see? Now compare Ephesians 1:10 with Psalm 2:8. Could the baptism of Jesus be a time of fulfillment?

There's More!

Please visit RickDPadgett.com where you'll find interactive online content and bonus articles related to the chapters in *Get Prayer and Get It All*.

---

3 The name used here, LORD, "Yahweh" or "I Am," is a perfect title for God that emphasizes His ALL.

5

GET PRAYER AND
GET THE SPIRIT

I choose a life of prayer because it is the only
way to invite the power of the Holy Spirit into my
circumstance.

Most of us have a way of declaring that spring has won the fight, once again driving away the gray kingdom of winter. As much as I don't like the dark days of winter, I think people who live in climates without seasons are missing something—the annual rituals. They never know the blissful release of shedding winter's lethargy and awakening to spring's optimism. The rite of spring reminds me to be intentional about life.

When it comes to spring rituals, tomatoes are my particular groundhog—my sure sign of spring. I *love* tomatoes. The Pacific Northwest rain may be pounding on my windows, but I get back at winter's darkest days with coffee and the glossy color photos of a seed catalogue devoted entirely to tomatoes. I read my copy and smirk at the cold soggy weather. I know tomatoes will prevail.

Twenty years of trial and error have produced three tomatoes that lead the charge against winter's tyranny: The Pink Brandywine, Dr. Wyche's Yellow, and the Amish Paste. These are the standard bearers of my tomato brigade. Each of them has proven indispensible in their loyal service to my table over the years.

The Pink Brandywine is known for its ability to hold all the elements of tomato essence together in a perfect blend of sugar and acid. The deep richness of this tomato is wrapped in a gorgeous pink exterior that often has light green stripes running down the shoulders of the fruit from the stem. To meet Pink Brandywine freshly picked on a warm late summer day is tomato nirvana. In fact, this tomato is so good she might tempt you to stop exploring the tomato world altogether. She is a jealous creature, whispering that nothing can be added to her perfection. That is, unless you happen to see the lovely auburn beauty in the next row.

The auburn beauty that catches your eye is Dr. Wyche's Yellow. The first thing you notice is she really isn't yellow. Dr. Wyche's starts the ripening process by turning yellow, but when conditions are just right Wyche's develops deep orange highlights, starting at the stem and progressing toward the blossom end of the tomato. When it comes to flavor this tomato makes its own rules. Wyche's takes the richness of the Pink Brandywine and transforms it into a melon-like experience. Even non-tomato people taste this tomato and shake their heads saying, "I had no idea a tomato could do that." Dr. Wyche's is in a class all her own.

The final member of my elite tomato SWAT team is the Amish Paste. After hearing the virtues of my two other favorites, you might be asking, "What could this tomato do to join the ranks?" The answer is *plenty*. Your first clue is in the name. The Amish people are really America's original "foodies." Our Amish friends were practicing organic heirloom *slow food* before anyone ever put a label on the movement. This is their tomato. In tomato tasting competitions the Amish Paste always places at or near the top.

The Amish has a long list of other virtues. First, she is a ruby-red beauty and a sweetheart, being a member of the sub-class labeled Ox Heart tomatoes. These tomatoes actually grow in the shape of a heart. Beneath her glossy gem-like exterior you'll find an especially meaty interior with small seeds. It cooks into a heavenly smooth sauce and chops into a life-changing salsa. When the winter doldrums set in, I simply reach for my secret supply of Amish Paste spaghetti sauce or crack open the Amish salsa for a reminder of last summer's final triumph; winter is now on notice that it will relinquish its power yet again.

I share my love of tomatoes to make a point. When you discover something really good, something that is compelling and sets new standards, you may want to keep looking. If you keep looking, you might find it has some incredible friends.

More Is Better

My journey into a life of prayer has certainly proved this principle of variety in numerous ways. What began as a simple aspiration to be near God has opened the way to endless surprises and discoveries. I'm learning that good things come in plural form. For me the centerpiece of this "plural goodness" in prayer has been watching my heart respond to ALL of the Trinity. Discovering the beauty of each member of the Trinity has been one of my main delights.

When you *Get It All* in prayer, you find the tri-unity of God the Father, God the Son, and God the Holy Spirit, ALL present to hear and advocate for and empower you. God's ALL is *all three persons*.

We've taken a brief look at how the life of prayer opens our hearts to God's ALL in His Son and God's ALL as our Father. This "dual goodness" of the Father and the Son is so irresistible I think it is important to challenge you that *there is still more*. In some ways, I may have saved the best for last.

Now we come to the third member of the Trinity, the Holy Spirit. In many ways, the Holy Spirit operates as the main connection between the ALL of God and the life of prayer.

In the language of a gardener, I would put it this way: If you really want God's ALL, you will never regret giving the Holy Spirit a preferred place in the garden of your life.

Variety Is the Spice of Prayer

During the late summer harvest, when it's time to put up my spaghetti sauce or salsa, every variety has its special place—even a special role. The Amish Paste makes a dreamy sauce, while Dr. Wyche's yellow is my choice for salsa. The vine-ripened Pink Brandywine is a solo star performer when raw, fresh and sliced. Nothing is needed to improve her flavor.

I would say, for a true gourmet experience in my kitchen, that *variety is my key ingredient*. The "more is better" principle offers a richer experience than any one member of my tomato trio could provide. We enjoy tomatoes because we enjoy a *variety* of tomatoes.

Prayer is like this when we involve all three members of the Trinity. In my early experiences in prayer I didn't always include the Holy Spirit. It's not far from what some of us experience even today. But now I know my key ingredient! When it comes to the simple recipe for prayer, we cannot afford to leave the Holy Spirit out. His special assignment is directly tied to prayer.

Romans 8 is Paul's treatise on living life in the Spirit. He especially emphasizes the *super-joining* of the Holy Spirit with prayer. *When we don't know what we ought to pray for, the Spirit helps us in our weakness;* [the Spirit] *intercedes for us through wordless groans; he searches our hearts and intercedes for God's people according to God's will* (Romans 8:26-27).

Don't miss what he just said: *We do not know what we ought to pray*. Even Paul had to admit he was sometimes stumped at the altar of prayer. After reading Romans 8:26-27, I half wonder if we would even know how to begin to pray--except as the Holy Spirit does His important work in, for and through us. What's humanly impossible, the Spirit makes more than possible, thankfully!

Jesus' Promise of More

Have you ever felt lonely in prayer? Have you felt as though you didn't know what to say or how to pray? Jesus knew we would feel that way, so He made a promise to His disciples. He promised they would never have to experience the isolation they feared would come if Jesus "left" them. So, Jesus promised to send another Comforter: *one just like me to come alongside you.*

Jesus was telling them (and us) about the key ingredient of more! He explained that Spirit-empowered prayer is the only prayer that invites God to be at our side. The Holy Spirit is God's ALL with us—His *fullness* in presence and power and help right alongside us.

Jesus never meant for us to pray alone. He sent the Holy Spirit on special assignment to conquer our isolation, to continue teaching us, to bolster and encourage us, and to bring the Kingdom of Heaven to earth—just as Jesus had done in His physical body here on earth.

Prayer is super-charged when we don't pray alone—when we agree with even one other person (Matthew 18:19-20). Prayer is also super-charged when the Spirit releases us from loneliness. Isn't that Jesus' promise to us? I will not leave you alone.

Jesus, the Spirit-filled Man

The surest way to test any theory about the faith life is to start with the life of Jesus. If we are learning how the Holy Spirit is uniquely central to the life of prayer, we should use the "Jesus test."

I start by revisiting the main storyline of Chapter 4 in this book. On the very first day of Jesus' public ministry, marked by His baptism, bystanders along the Jordan bore witness as Jesus joined prayer and the Holy Spirit. The Holy Spirit descended on Jesus at His baptism while He was praying (Luke 3:21-22). The God-man, standing at the biggest turning point of human history, asked God for more! He asked God for ALL. Jesus received the permanent indwelling presence of the Holy Spirit in the posture of prayer, an example that would be repeated over and over in His life and in the lives of His disciples.

It is interesting that Luke, as a New Testament author, seems to emphasize Jesus' Spirit-filled life more than any other writer. He is always showing us how Jesus followed the pattern established at His baptism—the pattern of a Spirit-filled ministry.

Jesus always joins with the Spirit during each key moment and challenge. He returned from the desert, after forty days of fasting and prayer, *in the power of the Spirit* (Luke 4:14). His first public sermon as Messiah begins by proclaiming *the Spirit of the Lord is upon me* (Luke 4:18).

Jesus is *full of joy and the Holy Spirit* during a prayer of thanksgiving (Luke 10:21), and moments later you read Jesus teaching that *the supreme request of prayer is the gift of the Holy Spirit* (Luke 11:9).

At the very end of His ministry, Jesus told His disciples that they should follow His example and instruction by waiting in prayer for the coming ALL of the Holy Spirit (Luke 24:49).

Luke's Gospel offers a marvelous narrative of Jesus, the Spirit-filled man.

By His words and example, Jesus taught us *how to join the Holy Spirit to a life of prayer*. He began His public life demonstrating it and ended His earthly ministry by commanding His followers to do the same.

The Disciples' Response

But did His disciples get His message? Let's flip over to the book of Acts, also authored by Luke, and see how they did.

The coming of the Holy Spirit at Pentecost was a mega-event. It's the final promised delivery of God's ALL on the doorstep of the new kingdom ushered in by Jesus Christ's life, death and triumphant resurrection. Only, we all know it wasn't a simple delivery; it was a tsunami of blessings. Nothing would be the same! Jesus had tried to explain this to the disciples, but nothing really could have prepared them for this day.

So, back to our question: Did the disciples follow Jesus' simple strategy to connect their lives to the powerful work of the Holy Spirit?

We can see that…

- They waited in prayer for the Holy Spirit (Acts 1:14; 2:1-4).

- They received the gift of tongues, which accompanied the outpouring of the Spirit, and often used it in their prayer life (1 Corinthians 14:2, 15, 26; Jude 20; Ephesians 6:18).

- They kept prayer in the middle of their daily practice (Acts 2:42; not surprisingly, the next seven verses contain five ALL words).

- When the Church encounters persecution, prayer resulted in an out-pouring of the Spirit (Acts 4:23-31).

- Peter and John went to the region of Samaria specifically to pray for the new believers there to receive the Holy Spirit (Acts 8:14-16).

- Ananias obeyed a vision directing him to lay hands on Paul and pray for Paul to be filled with the Holy Spirit, thus launching Paul's life and ministry (Acts 9:11,17-18).

- Paul travels to the city of Ephesus and prays for the believers to receive the Holy Spirit (Acts 19:2-6).

- The missionary movement is launched as the Church fasts and prays in the Holy Spirit (Acts 13:1-4).

So, how did the disciples do on their lessons? I would have to say they passed with high marks! They made the critical connection between the Holy Spirit and the practice of prayer demonstrated in the life of Jesus.

Just like Jesus, they lived and taught that prayer prepares the way for God's ALL—His unlimited power and resource—in the person of the Holy Spirit. Prayer is pivotal to receiving more—to receiving the fullness of what God has for you and me through the person and work of the Holy Spirit.

The Holy Spirit is Jesus' promised demonstration of God's presence and power with us. Prayer is literally super-charged by the release of the Holy Spirit.

* * * * *

When you're seated at a beautifully decorated table, preparing for a gourmet experience, more is always better. The pursuit of God's ALL always keeps us seeking more, and always whets our appetite for more.

Right now, take a moment to picture yourself invited to a beautifully decorated table offering a royal feast. At the table the Father, the Son, and the Holy Spirit are busy conversing. As you pray, *they invite you into their conversation.* In fact, they are planning a variety of experiences for you. The possibilities of working together begin to unfold and include an adventure for you!

Would you ignore any one of them as you participate in their conversation? In particular, would you leave out the One assigned to empower your adventure?

Prayer and the Holy Spirit cannot be divided in any way. There is only one way to "measure" the Holy Spirit and that is with God's measure of ALL. God is either fully with us or He is not.

The Holy Spirit is always with us in a life of prayer, but sometimes we neglect to notice Him at the table and include Him in our conversation.

I have tried praying without the Holy Spirit and it isn't fun. *Always ask God for more of the Holy Spirit; just like Jesus, He is the one we rely on in a life of prayer.*

* * * * *

A Scripture-based Interactive Prayer from John 14:25-26, 15:26-27 and 16:12-15

Precious Holy Spirit, please fill me and baptize me with a deposit of ALL You have for me. I want to receive the gift that Jesus promised to send so I will never be alone. Teach me to understand the power of Your love, the power of Your truth, and the necessity of You in my life. I reject any notion that I am an orphan, and I welcome Your Spirit of adoption in my life. Lead me to Jesus, reveal the Father's love to me, walk with me, and when I falter or forget please forgive me through the power of the blood of Jesus. He promised You would come to lead me and guide me and be my helper until His return. Fill me now and teach me how to pray, in the power of the Father, the Son, and the Holy Spirit. Amen.

Getting ALL In!

1. **Read John 14:25-26.** In verse 26 we see the Trinity intimately involved and in full agreement about the Holy Spirit's role in our lives. What two things did Jesus promise the Spirit would do? In what ways are the New Testament Gospels—Matthew, Mark, Luke and John—a fulfillment of that two-fold promise?

2. **Read John 15:26-27.** In verse 26 we again see the Trinity working in tandem. What two things did Jesus promise would happen after the Spirit came upon His disciples? In what ways is the book of Acts a direct or indirect fulfillment of that two-fold promise?

3. **Read John 16:12-13.** What two things did Jesus promise the Spirit would do? In what ways are the New Testament letters—Romans through Jude—a direct or indirect fulfillment of that two-fold promise?

4. **Read John 16:14-15.** In these two verses we see the Trinity again in full agreement. What two things did Jesus promise the Spirit would do? In what ways is the book of Revelation a fulfillment of that two-fold promise?

There's More!

Please visit RickDPadgett.com where you'll find interactive online content and bonus articles related to the chapters in *Get Prayer and Get It All*.

6

GET PRAYER AND
GET DESPERATION

I choose a life of prayer because it is the only way
to sustain desperation in my life.

I have a friend named Ed Bower. Our friendship is currently suspended because cancer destroyed his body. It seems odd, but his voice is clearer to me today than it was the last time we talked. Ed was a master of understatement. He never made a big deal about anything. I guess he had decided if something was important or funny it didn't need a drum roll. If you could manage any type of spontaneous expression or response from Ed you had just done something very unusual. I probably noticed this because we were so different in that respect.

Shortly before Ed left us, another friend asked if he could come along on my weekly visit to Ed. He and his wife graciously gave us the green light, even though they didn't know my friend. But I was nervous. As I ushered my friend next to Ed's bedside, I didn't know what to expect. I decided to sit back and let things take their course.

On some of those final days Ed was remarkably lucid and this was one of those days. After the small talk ran out, the only thing left was the stark reality of a dying man surrounded by his wife and seven children. I could see my friend was getting uneasy, so I nearly stepped in to intervene. Then something happened I will never forget.

Into the uneasy air of the room my friend asked a seemingly innocent question. He looked at Ed with genuine empathy and asked, "What days does your doctor come?"

Ed glanced his way. In his wonderful monotone voice he answered, "The doctor doesn't come anymore; it's just Jesus and me."

Ed's matter of fact response hit me like a stun grenade blasting my chest. I looked away, struck by an invisible blow. My head was spinning and I couldn't remember how to breathe. I don't even remember how I said goodbye; I think my friend prayed. I just remember slumping against the garage wall as I waited outside for my friend to say his goodbyes.

I was trying to understand what had just happened.

Instinctively I began to pray, *God, what is going on?*

God's response was immediate; I heard His quiet voice of authority speak: *This isn't about Ed. It's about you. What is true for Ed is true for you; it is always just you and Me.*

What I heard in those words has never left me. I saw myself trading places with Ed. I could make no distinction between his condition and mine.

It would take a long time to unwrap the gift that Ed slipped into my unsuspecting hands that day. It has been nine years, and I am still not sure I have seen the whole of it, but what I have seen shapes the rest of this chapter.

* * * * *

In the Ed Bower School

So, what do you call it when everybody else disappears except you and God? When it's just you and Him and nobody else—an audience of one? What is that called?

I looked for a single word to write at the top of my page, a title or a label for what had landed on my life. As I started to process my Ed Bower lesson, the word I chose was **desperation**.

In the faith life, *desperation* is the moment when you lose hope in man-made solutions to the big issues of life. You realize you have a God-sized problem.

You want "out of" this mess. You want "into" a future and a hope.

Your heart is forced to confront the big issues of life: death, disease, and disappointment; health and relationships; meaning and significance.

Desperation always hits there—when your deepest loves and hopes and dreams are frustrated or totally lost.

When we witness or experience tragic loss, and come face-to-face with a God-sized problem, it's a moment of desperation.

Then again, desperation also visits the crucible of wealth and success. It especially visits when someone "finally arrives" only to discover that their ticket "out of" a meaningless life or hopeless relationships can't be paid for with money, fame or power. It's the age-old hit of the '60s generation, sung by the Rolling Stones, "I can't get no satisfaction."

Desperation became a mega-word in my vocabulary when I realized God wants all that I am for all of Him at all times—both the good and desperate times. My friend, Ed, had nailed desperation with one simple comment: *It's just Jesus and me.*

In whatever circumstance of life you find yourself, eventually your life is reduced to an audience of one: *you and God.*

My short definition of desperation is this: *There is no "Plan B."*

Walking on the Edge of a Knife

Whether you are in the faith or out of faith, when desperation hits, it may feel like you are walking on the edge of a knife. Desperation can make you reckless. It points you outside the rules, even the rules ascribed to God.

Remember the woman who touched the hem of Jesus' garment? She had no business touching anyone. She was "unclean" by the standard of the Law, yet her desperation made her push past the normal protocol. When desperation settles on your life, you find your feet running headlong into the *anarchy* of desperation. You find yourself questioning the status quo and the standard procedures and their power over your life. Why? Because they are not working.

Just like the woman who touched Jesus garment, your desperate need for a real answer shifts your allegiance. The unquestioned protocol that once governed your reason can vaporize when you find yourself reaching for your only hope.

Desperation is an extremely dangerous moment in the human heart. Anyone who has been there knows a fine line exists between *desperation that leads to despair (and self-destruction)* and *desperation that leads to faith and life.* Desperation brings you to the crossroads of despair and faith.

In fact, desperation brings you to the Cross.

For all its perils, desperation remains the greatest prize of the faith life, the point of *decision* or *choosing*—the *turning point.* When you "win" this prize, every good thing that comes with faith is yours. Remember the end of the desperate woman's story?

The "Out Of" and "Into" Questions of Desperation

The long definition of desperation is being written each day in the story of my life, and in yours. It's the deconstructive process we each experience, in a wide variety of ways, leading us to our ALL moment—the moment of the ALL exchange. The ALL exchange is the choice to love and be loved with abandon. The ALL exchange is shameless—with nothing to lose and very little to give, it is ready to be loved in an undivided way, and it is ready to reciprocate with undivided love.

I believe the window on this understanding is why Ed could knock me to my knees from his sickbed. He was in the realm of ALL and I wasn't—at least, not yet.

The crucible of desperation brings us to the ALL moment by forcing us to face two tyrannical questions. Tyranny simply means these are not multiple choice questions: they are not about the search for knowledge and they don't participate in the democratic process. These questions visit our life to force a single conclusion.

If you pass through the narrowness of this moment you will find faith and life. If you reject the path of faith and life, you will never escape this narrow place. You will be "stuck"—back where you started, in your self-sufficiency, staring at death.

The first question we all face, in moments of desperation, is the "out of" question: "Who can get me out of here?" or "Who can save me from death?" When we are powerless to change our external circumstances, our heart is designed by a personal God to ask a person-directed question, "Who has the genuine power to rescue me?"

The echo of that question still resounds in the Apostle Paul's wrestling with his "wretched man"—the man who wants to choose *his own way* or *Plan B*. Paul wrestles with the same internal struggles we all face. In one loud cry as a prisoner to the law of sin Paul shouts, *"What a wretched man I am! Who will rescue me from this body of death?"* (Romans 7:24).

The "wretched man" will always wrestle for Plan B! But the tyranny of truth, God's jealous love for your heart, keeps pointing to surrender. The multiple choice answers fall off the page and point to one answer in the person of Jesus Christ—the One who has the ultimate power for your ultimate rescue.

The second question we all face, in moments of desperation, is "Who can make my life worth living?" When you lay in bed at night and your heart interrogates you, this is the second question of desperation. It's a question designed for an answer. Your questions may sound like this: Is there more to life? Am I really happy? Is my life really what I hoped it would be? Does my life have significance and meaning?

The "into" question is just as important as the "out of" question, but in many ways it is the more difficult of the two. These internal questions take a deep level of honesty about the condition of your heart and the allegiances of your heart. If you come up "empty" with an ultimate answer, this unmet inner longing will continue the search, always attempting to attach itself to someone or something of value. Since temporary things and people eventually disappoint our hearts, we will find ourselves revisiting this place until an ultimate answer for value is found.

I don't think any writer has yet approached both the heights and depths of the internal honesty written in the Psalms. For millennia people have turned to the Psalms to express their hearts' inward questions about meaning and longing.

In Psalm 73:25-26 the psalmist, Asaph, settles on the answer to our second question with poetic language.

> *25 Whom have I in heaven but you?*
> *And earth has nothing I desire besides you.*
> *26 My flesh and my heart may fail,*
> *but God is the strength of my heart*
> *and my portion forever.*

You may not notice it at first, but Asaph recognized what I've labeled a "tyranny of truth." He asks, "Whom have I in heaven but you?"

Then he dives right into the ALL-exchange, saying, in essence, "The external circumstances around me may not go well, but God fulfills my desire and satisfies the longings of my heart."

When we finally wave the white flag and surrender to the tyranny of truth, once the dust settles in the external and internal battlefields of our life, the overwhelming wisdom and kindness of God is waiting. It finally dawns on us that Ed was right. The only answer is the only One who has conquered death and desire.

The external circumstances and internal questions of desperation are not appointed by God to punish us or exclude us from God's mercy. The questions of desperation point all of us to God's ALL in one man—the man Christ Jesus. This is the story behind our common journey of desperation, it is the big story of human history, and Ed summed it up in just five words, "It's just Jesus and me." Thanks, Ed.

The "Out of" and "Into" Prayers of Desperation

You alone have a unique vantage point for reading this chapter, depending on when and how you have experienced the long definition of desperation that is *your story*.

Whether your view of desperation is fresh or faded or in the future, you can choose to practice for desperation now. That way, when it visits you or those you love, you will know how to stand. You will find rescue and refuge.

Now, why am I encouraging you to "Get Desperation"? And how do we practice for it?

I'm encouraging you to revisit the place where I found Ed in his home hospice. I'm encouraging you to get to the place in your heart where *it's just Jesus and you*, every day. That can only happen in prayer, to an audience of One.

Prayer takes you daily through the deconstructive process of man-made solutions. Prayer invites God's kindness to sift your heart. Prayer answers desperation's questions every day, taking you "out of" your lack of resources and bringing you "into" the Father's house where God's ALL now is your resource.

You might agree with me that life itself can be a desperate proposition. We will always face desperation at some level, with or without faith. But I believe desperation is a gift God uses to lead us back to the Father's house. I believe desperation is a friend to be welcomed, even if it can be annoying and painful.

The Lord's kindness convinces me that I no longer have the power to save myself or to manufacture meaning for my existence. In the midst of desperation, God's kindness leads us to the place of decision and a place of rescue. His kindness demolishes every obstacle to your heart. It may feel like a harsh judgment at the time, but His kindness judges every attempt to answer the "out of" and "into" questions apart from Jesus Christ.

When desperation visits your life, it has two jobs to do: the work of emptying ("out of") and of filling ("into"). If you surrender to the emptying work of desperation, eventually the tide turns and you come into a season of unprecedented filling—enjoying God's ALL as never before.

So, how do you pray for this?

Two One-word Prayers of Desperation

I see the vocabulary of desperation embedded in two familiar, biblical one-word prayers. We all know them, yet I think of them as the secret passwords of faith. After all, they have power to open your heart to all the riches of Jesus Christ. They are the foundation of all real prayer.

The "out of" prayer of desperation is "Mercy!"

The "into" prayer of desperation is "Abba!"

Beginning with these words, God will respond to you and fill every part of your life. These two one-word prayers are the irreducible link between the crucible of desperation and entering into God's ALL.

Mercy: The Prayer of Rescue

Consider the power and the hope in the cry "Mercy!" called out to a merciful God. Over and over again, the psalmist, David, runs into God's arms equipped only with this one-word prayer.4 Not surprisingly, it reverberates throughout the rest of the Scriptures.

> *The LORD has heard my cry for mercy; the LORD accepts my prayer (Psalm 6:9).*

> *It does not, therefore, depend on man's desire or effort, but on God's mercy (Romans 9:16).*

> *Once you were not a people, but now you are the people of God; once you had not received mercy, but now you have received mercy (1 Peter 2:10-11).*

"Mercy!" is the prayer that God hears and lifts us out of the pit.

4 To read more see Psalm 28:2, 28:6, 31:22, 86:6, 116:1, 130:2, and 140:6.

"Mercy!" is the cry of my heart before the cross of Jesus Christ, knowing I have done nothing to justify His reckless, crazy love.

"Mercy!" is the confession that I can add nothing to what Jesus Christ has done and relinquishing my futile attempts at self-defense.

"Mercy!" is the desperate faith cry that abandons every human resource and throws itself upon God's riches.

"Mercy!" is the miracle of miracles delivered to our lives in a single-word prayer.

At our point of desperation, God promises to answer the prayer for "Mercy!" and sets us up for our second one-word prayer.

Abba: The Prayer of Adoption

"*Abba!*" is both a prayer and a declaration in one word. The "Abba" prayer is specifically enabled by the Holy Spirit to break the enemy's claim on your life and establish God's ownership. So, Abba is a redeeming prayer! **Abba redeems your experience of desperation, giving it meaning and establishing your new identity and all the resources that go with it.**

> *The Spirit you received does not make you slaves, so that you live in fear again; rather, the Spirit you received brought about your adoption to sonship. And by him we cry, "Abba, Father." The Spirit himself testifies with our spirit that we are God's children (Romans 8:15).*

> *Because you are his sons, God sent the Spirit of his Son into our hearts, the Spirit who calls out, "Abba, Father." So you are no longer a slave, but God's child; and since you are his child, God has made you also an heir (Galatians 4:6).*

With this single-word prayer, "*Abba,*" we cross the threshold into the Father's house, and into a life of purpose and belonging and resource. As seen in Jesus' parable of the prodigal son, "*Abba!*" declares we are leaving the pit of despair, only to discover the Father is joyously restoring our fellowship as His son or daughter.

"*Abba!*" is the prayer of a rescued heart declaring to God, "*You have made my life worth living!*"

"*Abba!*" is both a request to fill our deepest desire and the satisfaction of that desire.

"*Abba!*" is the declaration of a heart set free from self-sufficiency, finding refuge and acceptance as a beloved son or daughter.

The single-word cry of *"Abba!"* reveals the universal longing of every heart to know, *"Now I know why I was created and where I am going."*

"Abba!" a single-word prayer claiming our *identity* and breaking both isolation and fear in the human heart. There is no greater joy or freedom than the joy and freedom of secure sons and daughters of God.

No one else but the Holy Spirit can teach us this prayer, and no one else but the Father can answer it.

* * * * *

In these two single-word prayers, our hearts acknowledge Jesus Christ as the perfect Savior and the Father's beloved Son.

In the simplicity of these two single-word prayers our hearts renounce pride and idolatry. This double heart cry is like a two-edged sword, cutting our ties to a man-made religion of works and doubt, leaving only grace and the Holy Spirit.

In two single-word prayers the fear of death is conquered by resurrection, and the emptiness of isolation is conquered by the Father's love.

In just two words—"Mercy!" and *"Abba!"*—desperation and prayer are joined to bring God's kingdom to your heart and to fill every part of your life with His love and provision.

If we submit to the gift of desperation, we will be joined to a life of prayer—abandoning man-made solutions, finding mercy, and receiving our inheritance as God's child. Because desperation opens the door for Jesus, desperation and prayer are inseparable.

"Get desperation" and your heart will be prepared for the fullness of God's ALL in your life. Desperation is the greatest prize of the faith life. Win this prize and every good thing that comes with faith is yours. Miss this and life in Jesus will remain a mystery.

Why wait any longer?

If Ed was here I know what he would say.

"It's just Jesus and me."

* * * * *

A Scripture-based Interactive Prayer from Psalm 88

Abba, Father, please have mercy on me. You are the only One who can save me. I cry out day and night to you alone. I feel overwhelmed by life. Sometimes I wonder if death may not be too far away. Other times I wonder if death might not be better. I've lost so much. I've been hurt so deeply. Nothing is going my way. Life seems to have turned against me. I've been pounded down so hard and so often. And yet I know there is One who can turn the tables, One who stood in the darkest day of human history and turned it into the greatest demonstration of Your mercy. My hope is in Him, and I pray in His name, the strong and unfailing name of Jesus. Amen.

Getting ALL In!

1. **Psalm 88 is literally called "A Psalm of Desperation."** Except for the opening line, the entire psalm is negative. It was written by a friend of King David, Heman the Ezrahite, who helped lead the nation in worship. His song of lament is included in the book of Psalms for a reason, but that reason escapes most contemporary readers. After all, verse after verse shows the psalmist is depressed. How do you think God sees such desperation? What does that tell you about your own story of desperation?

2. **How do we best respond in the midst of desperate circumstances?** Back up from Psalm 88 and glance over Psalm 77, written by Asaph, another friend of King David. In Psalm 77:7-9 we find six questions we may ask in times of desperation. In 77:13 we find the answer to such questions. What is the answer? Is it a satisfactory answer to your own story of desperation?

3. **Read Psalm 18, and then Psalm 6,** both written by David before he became king. What do you learn from these psalms about talking with God when you're desperate? What do you learn about God's mercy?

4. **The genealogy of King David is traced through Ruth and Naomi.** How did each woman respond in the midst of her desperation? What does it tell you about God's ways with the desperate, destitute, forsaken, and bereaved?

7

GET PRAYER AND
GET YOUR ANSWER

*I choose a life of prayer because it is the only way
to see God act on my behalf.*

I am the last of five children. My mother, like her mother before her, had
five children, three boys and two girls, the youngest being a son. Predictably,
my mom's youngest brother was my favorite uncle. We were kindred spirits,
having both survived the superior fire power of older siblings by shamelessly
exercising our status as "Mom's favorite." My older siblings taunted me as a
mama's boy, yet they gave me no other choice. I was on the bottom of the food
chain holding only one trump card, and I played it often.

There was one exception to my sibling's broad disgust toward my favored status: one situation when they laid down their animosity to include me in their
council, one circumstance when they embraced my "favored" status. When
they called me into their secret congress it meant only one thing: *they wanted
something from mom.* I knew deep down that their motives were tainted, but
the exhilaration of being included with the "big kids" carried me past any
moral reservations. When they came knocking with one of their schemes, I
was ready.

These "special operations," were complicated by two factors. First, my mom
was a single parent. In one tragic afternoon in 1968 my mom was thrust into
an unwanted role. It was brutal. In the 1960s "single mom" was not a social
class for women; she felt like a social outcast. As a result, the second compli-
cating factor was poverty. Going it alone, overwhelmed and underfunded, she
tended to be a little grumpy—especially when someone came around asking
for something extra out of her thin resources.

This made my job as Chief Negotiator, on behalf of the dependents, extremely
tricky. To aggravate mom's ever-present touchiness about our lean reserves, my
brothers and sisters invariably hatched their plans on Friday night. It was a
chronic case of bad timing. Fridays were the days when *other folks*—who had

resources and a good reason—went out to celebrate. My mom had neither and she didn't go out; instead, she went to bed early.

The final stage of negotiations was always the same. My brothers and sisters would hatch their plans in the back bedroom and then force me out to the family room while they hid in the hallway. Their idea of brotherly affection was to throw me into the fiery volcano of our mom's desperation, while waiting like cowards in the hallway for the grumbling goddess to pass judgment.

To our amazement, it almost always worked! My mom still loved to say yes to me, and would even reach for her purse and extract her sacrificial mite to four muffled cheers in the hallway. For five minutes on a rare Friday night, I was a hero.

Or so I thought. Once they extracted the cash from my "favored hand," I promptly returned to the untouchable caste. They wouldn't even sit with me at the movie. Such was my early life as the youngest child.

Being a little brother isn't glamorous, but it sometimes has its advantages.

Learning What I Needed to Learn

The Scriptures contain many stories about younger brothers. It wasn't until much later in life that I understood my "early training" as a baby brother had strategic value. This understanding came in my twenties, after reading the many Bible narratives that pay special honor to younger brothers.

Typically, younger brothers are unlikely candidates for power, position, and favor. Normally, they are far more likely to endure scorn and false accusations than praise. Yet I enjoyed reading the stories of younger brothers like Jacob and Joseph and David, the youngest brother chosen to be a king. I delighted in God's "soft spot" for those of us born somewhere down the ladder. And I always asked the question, "Why?" *Why would God choose and use the younger brother?*

My answer? In every story I see a consistent message and overarching principle: *God's lack of concern for human protocol.* His finger repeatedly pointing to this indelible fact: the big issues of life are not solved by man-made rules or human effort.

The biggest application of this principle is that no one, firstborn or last born, can add anything to God's love and favor—His *good will*—which He expressed to us in Jesus Christ. We do not need to rely on *any* particular protocol or status to achieve God's special favor; we only need to receive His favor by faith in His Son. No one, firstborn or last born, can add anything to what Jesus did for each us.

The younger brother narratives teach us that God doesn't favor any particular outward circumstance. Instead, He favors the individual inward stance. God is big enough to make every one of us, His sons and daughters, "the favorite."

I believe that every biblical narrative has a great reward—a gem or a prize we can add to our storehouse. The younger brother narratives reward us with confidence. Our confidence in preferential treatment isn't based on social protocol; it is founded in the Father's immense delight that we are His son or daughter.

What this means is that each of us can open our Father's wardrobe, just like Joseph, and discover a coat of many colors with our name on it. One has your name embroidered inside the collar.

God never intended for any of us to be less than His favorite.

Getting Dressed for Prayer

The repeated biblical narrative about the younger brother has huge implications for anyone attempting to create a meaningful definition of prayer. *Prayer is nothing less than daily putting on our many-colored coat.* It is the surest litmus of how we perceive God's favor in our lives. If we fail to we see ourselves clothed in God's favor, we will stand out in the hallway just like my older siblings.

If we don't come to God in prayer as His favorite, soon we won't come at all. If we learn to put on our coat and relish God's incredible favor toward us, however, our hearts will be bold and confident to come to Him with all of our requests.

Learning What I Needed to Unlearn

I find it fascinating that Jesus was quick to acknowledge our wrong perceptions of God and the difficulty this creates in our prayer life. So Jesus zeroed in on that perception and taught His disciples a parable to show them that they should always pray and not give up (Luke 18:1). He knew that most of us begin our faith journey thinking God is grumpy. We see Him as an unjust judge

(Luke 18:1-8), an unreasonable landlord (Luke 16:1-8), or an uncooperative neighbor (Luke 11:5-8).

Jesus didn't even bother trying to talk us out of these misconceptions. He simply used the disciple's misconceptions as ammunition! Essentially, Jesus said, "even grumpy people can be persuaded." I found His examples increased my confidence as I went through the process of losing my "grumpy God" outlook.

Jesus accepts our difficulty embracing favored status. At the same time, He goes right on wearing His coat of many colors. In prayer, He repeatedly speaks to God as His loving heavenly Father. *A huge lesson*! He didn't argue us into being a favorite. Instead, He demonstrated it for us.

Have you ever thought of wearing the coat of God's favor as a militant act? Your enemy doesn't like it! Your coat automatically confronts and rejects what the enemy offers you as substitutes for favor such as shame, blame, pride, and self-effort.

You might be surprised at how long your own list of "disqualifiers" is, and how committed you are to preserving your "sub-favorite" status.

I challenge you to now see your Father standing by holding your multi-colored jacket. He is gentle, but insistent. He knows it can be a scary step for you. He also knows that once you wear your coat, there is no going back. Maybe this is why Jesus didn't bother arguing the point; instead, He demonstrated it. He knew the Father joyfully gets His kids dressed.

"Me? God's favorite?" Because it's true, I have resolved to wear my coat every day without fail. Then again, I have all but given up trying to defend God's decision to dress me in such ridiculous extravagance. I have told Him I feel way overdressed, but He doesn't listen.

I can't wear your coat of favor. I won't argue whether you are God's favorite. Instead, I will simply stand dressed up and embarrassed, holding the door to the dressing room. The rest is between you and your Father.

Moving Our Prayers Out of the Hallway

As a young believer I fell in love with John 13-17. It's where Jesus Christ shares His heart with us in the final hours before His arrest and crucifixion. In this private gathering, Jesus focuses on preparing His followers for what is about to happen. You can feel the intense emotion final hours always hold.

It was just before the Passover Festival. Jesus knew that the hour had come for him to leave this world and go to the Father. Having loved his own who were in the world, he now showed them the full extent of his love (John 13:1).

Within the confines of time and space and His disciples' limited understanding, Jesus begins to unfurl the Kingdom of Heaven before their eyes. With a singular focus, He gives them words to sustain them through the crucible of the next few days. He loved them intensely and He called them *His own who were in the world*. These chapters are a "close-up" shot of His love and leadership.

Several themes shaped this meeting, but the biggest one is the fact that Jesus knew He was leaving. He knew the laws of love. He knew that separation was a direct contradiction of love's first impulse to be together, to be *with us*. Jesus wanted to help His disciples bridge this contradiction, so He gave them three mega-promises to build a bridge.

First, He told them the separation was only temporary. He would certainly return; love could tolerate nothing less (John 14:1-3).

Second, He told them the Holy Spirit would more than "fill the gap" created by His absence. Sending the Holy Spirit was the ultimate "love intervention" to deal with the contradiction of Jesus leaving.

A third mega-promise follows closely on the heels of these first two.

Jesus' Third Mega-promise

Right next to these first two mega-promises, Jesus places yet another mega-promise. He offers a third pillar of hope to sustain His disciples in the midst of the fierce storms about to break upon their lives.

It is the promise of answered prayer.

Five times Jesus repeats this promise, placing it right next to the promise of His second coming and the outpouring of the Holy Spirit. In His "theology of love," this promise was equal in importance to His return to consummate human history, and the dramatic events of the day of Pentecost. Five times He places it in this lofty company.

And I will do whatever you ask in my name, so that the Father may be glorified in the Son (John 14:13).

You may ask me for anything in my name, and I will do it (John 14:14).

You did not choose me, but I chose you and appointed you so that you might go and bear fruit—fruit that will last—and so that whatever you ask in my name the Father will give you (John 15:16).

Very truly I tell you, my Father will give you whatever you ask in my name (John 16:23).

Until now you have not asked for anything in my name. Ask and you will receive, and your joy will be complete (John 16:24).

Jesus couldn't have made it more obvious: answered prayer is not optional. Answered prayer isn't for an elite few or "super spiritual" prayer warriors; it is the baseline defining experience for every believer. No believer is excused from answered prayer as a first-hand reality. None of us are allowed to hide in the hallway. That kind of prayer life will not sustain our hearts when we encounter challenging circumstances.

Stop to consider *what* Jesus is saying and *when* Jesus is saying it—in the crisis hour, in the final test of His earthly ministry, in His closest relationships. In this moment Jesus places answered prayer in equal company to His second coming and the indwelling Holy Spirit.

Can we all stop and admit that is not how we look at answered prayer? We have all heard passionate arguments over end-times doctrine and the work of the Holy Spirit. Christians engage in debate over these two doctrines with fiery zeal. Yet, in over three decades of my faith journey, I have never heard a voice of passion speak with equal zeal about the "doctrine of answered prayer."

Yet, here it is, right before our eyes. Jesus repeats the doctrine of answered prayer in this compressed moment of crisis, when only the big stuff gets stage time.

Jesus taught one consistent message regarding prayer: *God is inclined to answer even though we are not inclined to ask.*

But we can ask. We must ask! We must set our eyes on the prize: a consistent pattern of visible answers to specific prayers. Jesus intended for His disciples to go right on asking the Father just as if He were physically present with them. Essentially, He told them, "Nothing is going to change in regard to prayer."

Does this cause you to question your own prayer life? Are you willing to leave behind any definition of prayer that does not include visible answers to specific prayers? Are we all willing to give up our escape clause, "if it be Your will"?

How long until I admit that answered prayer is God's will!

Answered prayer is essential to our baseline spiritual health. It is central to Jesus' definition of a disciple. Until we reach this critical conclusion, we will never experience a life of answered prayer.

Where Do We Start?

Jesus always prayed to the Father. He wore the coat of His Father's favor and mentioned it often. When He prayed, He prayed from the position of relationship, a favored son. Jesus always initiated prayer from this place and received God's answers—just as we are to initiate prayer with our "coat on" and receive God's answers too.

In some ways, I was lucky. I have a wealth of experience being the baby brother and being forced to ask my mom for favors. With four cattle prods at your back in the hallway, you would too. I developed the boldness to ask because I couldn't bear facing the consequences of not asking.

Allow me to walk you through to the "prize" of visible answers to specific prayers.

First, we want get into relationship with the Father as a favored son or daughter. We must always start with the truth of our rightful identity over our résumé of failure, disappointment, and disqualifications. God is a loving Father who eagerly waits to hear our voice.

Next, we want to follow Jesus' advice to be persistent and not give up on our requests when we don't receive on the first or second try. Persistence tries our motives and sifts out selfish want from true need and provision for others.

Lastly, we want to encourage ourselves with Jesus' own promise of answered prayer when we ask in His name. He modeled persistence by repeating this promise five times in His final moments with the disciples.

What encourages persistence in prayer until we see specific visible answers?

- Be specific and be sure to write down the details of each request.

- Learn the childlike exercise of repeating yourself. (I call this "pestering" God.)

- Ask God to give you a written Scripture to anchor your requests.

- Don't give up. Unanswered prayers are painful, but abandoning faith in a God who promised to answer is lethal.

- Remember to go back and write down the specific visible answer, the date, the circumstances, and your words of thanksgiving.

Few have aspired to a life of visible answered prayer more than Andrew Murray, author of the classic, *With Christ in the School of Prayer.* Here is a key paragraph by Murray, written more than a century ago, put into slightly more contemporary language.

> He (Jesus) wants to teach us **what in all Scripture is considered the chief thing in prayer: the assurance that prayer will be heard and answered.** Observe how He uses words which mean almost the same thing, and each time repeats the promise distinctly: you will receive, you will find, the door will be opened to you; and then gives us ground for such assurance in the law of the kingdom: he who asks receives, he who seeks finds, he who knocks will find the door opened to him. We cannot but feel how, in this six-fold repetition, He wants to impress deep on our minds this one truth, that **we may and must most confidently expect an answer to our prayer. Next to the revelation of the Father's love, there is, in the whole course of the school of prayer, not a more important lesson than this: Everyone who asks receives.**

* * * * *

A Scripture-based Interactive Prayer from Psalm 31:19

Father, I read out loud the confession of the psalmist, "How abundant are the good things that you have stored up for those who fear you, that you bestow in the sight of all, on those who take refuge in you." When I read these words I sometimes feel as if I am the only one who experiences unanswered prayers. I honestly wonder if my prayers even make a difference. All I can say is I am willing to start again. Teach me to pray in a way that produces visible answers. I want to experience the overwhelming joy of knowing that You hear and act on my behalf. I want to learn the power of praying as a favorite. I want to be the first one in line because I know how much You enjoy answering my prayers. I choose Your invitation to pray over my résumé of unanswered prayers. Thank you so much for the example of Jesus who leads us into

a life of answered prayer. It is because of Him that I come to start anew, to discover
what He said was so important, the experience of specific answered prayer. Amen.

Getting ALL In!

1. **One way to "get prayer" is to put on God's favor.** This requires using
   your imagination and it starts with remembering that God is your Father,
   and that you are His favored son or daughter. Close your eyes and picture
   yourself being helped into your coat of favor by your heavenly Father.
   (I think of the Masters golf jacket given each year by the previous year's
   champion.) How does it feel? What are your emotions as you put it on?
   What do you want to tell your heavenly Father?

2. **What part does wearing the many-colored coat of favor** play when
   you are processing the disappointment of unanswered prayer?

3. **Is it easier to remember unanswered or answered prayers?** Why? I
   encourage you to consider keeping a prayer journal. It doesn't have to
   be a literal journal. You can even put sticky notes in your Bible as long as
   the basic information is included. Simply make a short note of the prayer
   specifics and date, and then the answer and date.

8

GET PRAYER AND
GET THE WORD

I choose a life of prayer because prayer is the only way to experience God's ALL in the written Scriptures.

I have always been fascinated by weapons. My lifelong interest parallels most books on the history of warfare and self-defense. Like the weapon-loving tribe who preceded me, I found my first weapon by picking up a rock. My earliest memory of the power in a hand-launched rock was on the receiving end. A neighbor kid threw a large stone into an open pit—my open pit. I looked up just in time to see the sun disappear as the rock hit me square in the face. That was my first broken nose. It was also the first time I remember thinking, "Wow, there's a lot of blood in a nose!"

My fascination with weapons grew, so I dutifully followed in the footsteps of my weapon-toting ancestors by adding sticks to my arsenal. Although initially swung as clubs, I soon got around to sharpening some into spears. I practiced launching and sticking my spears into various objects, learning just the right touch and balance. Fortunately nobody's nose ever got in the way of my early experiments.

The next addition to my arsenal? I discovered string. A good piece of string proved to be a game-changer. My inspiration likely came from B-rated Cowboy and Indian movies where I saw the genius of the bow and arrow. A simple piece of string could transform two modestly dangerous sticks into a weapon that could kill a buffalo. At least, that's what the movie led me to believe.

My fascination with bows would last for a long time. Even after I had the resource and proper ID to acquire more sophisticated weapons, I still returned to the simple genius of the bow and arrow. I saw the bow as the secret behind all weapon advancements—the principle of combination.

Advancing the effectiveness of any weapon is contingent upon discovering new ways to combine and maximize their individual components. New combinations of the rock, stick, and string drove the art of war for centuries. Bows, slings, catapults, trebuchets, and a host of medieval weapons were just combinations of these three basic elements.

You may be wondering, "What does all this have to do with the life of faith, and in particular the practice of prayer?"

I have discovered that the principle of combination to maximize the effectiveness of military weapons, also works to maximize the power of our prayer life. In the same way a piece of string can turn two sticks into a buffalo-killing machine, joining our prayers to other elements of our God-given arsenal exponentially multiplies their power and effectiveness.

The main combination I would like to explore in this chapter is the joining of the voice of prayer with the written Scriptures.

In the theater of prayer God has given His people two powerful weapons. Individually they wield enormous influence, but when combined they become almost limitless in their power and authority. The first is well-known and universally appreciated, and long considered to be the single most effective weapon in the Christian arsenal: the written word of the Scriptures.

The second is well-known and chronically under-appreciated. Although the Bible refers to its enormous power, most of us don't honor it *by practice* as a significant asset. I am talking about the human voice in prayer.

When the written Scriptures and the human voice are combined in prayer, God responds in unprecedented fashion, activating His unlimited authority and resource.

Although I had heard about this combination fairly early in my faith journey, it took an embarrassingly long time before I actually began to practice this combination.

Once I saw the genius of this partnership, it became much like my experience with bow and arrow. To me it represents the core genius and strategy that God has put in place to weaponize His church.

Consider the following Scriptures to underscore the power of the *spoken* word, and the power of the *written* word.

> *The tongue has the power of life and death, and those who love it will eat its fruit (Proverbs 18:21).*

> *Their mouths lay claim to heaven, and their tongues take posses-*

sion of the earth (Psalm 73:9).

The words I have spoken to you—they are full of the Spirit and life (John 6:63).

Jesus replied, "You are in error because you do not know the Scriptures or the power of God" (Matthew 22:29).

But we will devote ourselves to prayer and the ministry of the Word (Acts 6:4).

Take the helmet of salvation and the sword of the Spirit, which is the word of God. And pray in the Spirit on all occasions with all kinds of prayers and requests (Ephesians 6:17-18).

By joining vocal prayer with Scripture, we have a supreme example of a dynamic partnership. The mix of the written words of Scripture and the spoken words of our prayers increases the caliber of our prayers and opens a floodgate from God's throne and His storehouse into our circumstance.

Divide the Word and prayer and you will limit their effectiveness—perhaps forfeiting untapped possibilities (even though each will always retain its intrinsic value).

Join them and—like bow and string—they release exponential help to our lives. Once the Word of God and the human voice are joined in prayer, there is no going back; it becomes impossible to consider one without the other. Once you learn to pray with your Bible open, it will never again be just a book to read or study. Once the words of Scripture come alive in your prayers, you will never be content to pray any other way.

We find beautiful examples, in both the Old and New Testaments, of Scripture-based prayers. Everyone who prayed this way exercised faith by laying claim to the words originally spoken by others, to others, in other places, often in other centuries. Joshua, Hannah, and Samuel offered up Scripture-based prayers. So did David, Solomon, Elijah, Habakkuk, Jeremiah, Ezekiel, Daniel, Nehemiah, Ezra, Zachariah, Mary, Paul, and other believers (both well-known and unnamed). Those Scripture-based prayers had a dramatic impact, joining heaven and earth in spectacular fashion.

Perhaps Jesus had this kind of faith in mind when He told His disciples that in order to be *a disciple in the kingdom of heaven* they should learn to *bring out of His storeroom new treasures as well as old* (Matthew 13:52).

The Prayer that Activates Angels and Directs Human History

Daniel shows us how this kind of prayer works when he is moved by the words of Jeremiah and Moses. In Daniel 9 he prays these words for himself and for the nation of Israel. Daniel moved the hand of God by joining Scriptures with the spoken voice of prayer, so much so that the archangel Gabriel visited him saying, "As soon as you began to pray, an answer was given." Daniel skillfully used Scripture-based prayer as a direct line to God's heart and God's undivided attention. Daniel's prayer opened the way for the whole nation to reconnect to God's purposes.

Is this enough to get your attention?

Are you interested in this kind of prayer life?

The Prayer that Defines the Greatest Moment of History

What's more, in Jesus' greatest hour of need, He prayed the Scriptures. In the final moments of His passion He prayed Psalm 22 (Mark 15:34). *The perfect Man uses a Scripture-based prayer as the perfect end to His perfect life.* He placed Himself into the very words of the Psalm, using language a thousand years old to express the deepest emotions ever experienced in human history.

If nothing else had been said on this subject of praying Scripture, the final moments of Jesus' perfect life should convince us to give serious thought to this matter. Consider the events immediately released by Jesus' final words: the Temple veil is torn in two, rocks are split, and many are raised from the dead (Matthew 27:50-54). That's power!

Let's never forget: *God's power* shows up when we pray His Word.

The Prayer that Empowers the New Church

In Acts 4:23-31 the brand-new Church experienced its first serious persecution. The early believers were at a critical crossroads. As they gathered to pray in the midst of this crisis, how do they give voice to their circumstances and emotions? How do they bring unity and clarity to their corporate voice of prayer?

They did exactly what Jesus did—they fell back on the Scriptures to guide their hearts in prayer. Specifically, the first Christians took up Psalm 2, one of the prophetic Psalms about Jesus Christ and the clash of worldly kingdoms. The earliest brothers and sisters in Christ remembered the changing power structure prophesied in Psalm 2—and saw themselves living in these words.

When they entered into prayer, appealing to God's intervention on the basis of His Word, their prayer released something powerful within the heart of God—and they experienced a direct manifestation of God's kingdom. "After they prayed, the place where they were meeting was shaken. And they were all filled with the Holy Spirit and spoke the Word of God boldly."

When God's people join the written words of Scripture with the spoken word of prayer, He responds in a dramatic demonstration of His undivided attention. That is a pretty good advertisement for Scripture-based prayer! It is simple and yet it is a game-changer.

A Closer Look at Joining of the Voice of Prayer and the Written Word

If you are like me, you can't help but wonder why this simple approach to prayer can yield such huge benefits. Let's consider the reasons why it has such a dramatic impact.

First, the written words of Scripture give us a hard focus for our prayers. Faith requires an object on which to fix its attention and the Scriptures are perfectly suited to this assignment.

Choosing a "hard focus" on Scripture literally shapes our prayer. Most Scripture-based prayers are driven by the fact that our inner or outer circumstances don't measure up to the passage we are praying. As we fix our eyes on the passage, the Holy Spirit can shed light on the contradiction. At the same time, His power enables your life and your circumstance to come into agreement with the Scriptures.

By simply fixing our attention on the written words, we uniquely position our hearts to choose faith and promise over unbelief and circumstance. This is the engine of Scripture-based prayer.

Second, the words and emotions recorded in the Scriptures can be a *launching point* for building our own "lover's conversation with God."

The movie *Finding Forrester* (Columbia Pictures) is one of my favorite illustrations about the value of launching points. Jamal, a young writer, stumbles into a mentor relationship with a reclusive and embittered author named William

Forrester. In a pivotal scene, Jamal is asked to sit and write under his mentor's observation. The result is predictable. The inexperienced writer freezes, unable to produce a single phrase.

After several agonizing minutes Forrester does an amazing thing. He goes to his files and pulls out an old story of his own. He props it up in front of his student and commands him to write. As Jamal begins to object to copying his mentor's work, the wise teacher says, "Only copy the words until your own take over." Reluctantly the young man obeys. In a few minutes he is no longer looking at the old, but he is deeply involved in his own creative process.

The Scriptures can do the exact same thing for us as we journey into the intimacy of prayer. Often we don't know how or where to start. If we will follow the old writer's strategy we will discover that the Scripture has an infinite capacity to "prime the pump" for those of us who need to be mentored into the life of prayer.

Of course, it is simple to the point of offending our pride. Be warned! This is nothing more than the childlike exercise of tracing our fingers over the words of Scripture "until your own take over."

Another clue to the power of praying the Scriptures is found in the principle of tithing. Tithing is returning to God a portion of what He has given to us. In the act of returning a portion to God, we are affirming and activating God's ownership of the whole. We are inviting Him to come and take possession of everything He has given, to bless it and add His presence to everything He has put in our lives.

Praying the Scriptures takes a small part of the whole gift of written revelation and offers it back to God. We are affirming that all of the Scriptures are His, and that these Scriptures flow from His continuous desire to speak into our lives.

When we pray the Scriptures, we are agreeing that God is not silent, and that His love will not be silent. The moment you make this kind of offering you step into the realm of God's ALL, and specifically step into His promises concerning the benefits of tithing.

There is an overflow from this kind of prayer not found in any other kind of prayer.

What's in it for you? Praying the Scriptures is an act of faith that brings the Kingdom and God's ALL into your life and circumstances. Praying the Scriptures has huge practical consequences for the life of prayer. If this is true, you and I will want to give a high priority to praying out loud with our Bibles open. We will long to join our Bible reading and studying to Scripture praying.

What's more, if we learn to pray the Scriptures, then much of the previous awkwardness and wandering of our prayers will be replaced with the power and clarity of God pouring out truth through our prayers. What a wonderful trade!

Without a doubt, when the written Scriptures and the human voice are combined in prayer, they become almost limitless in their power and authority. They become mighty weapons advancing the Kingdom of God in the seen and unseen worlds.

Time to Open Up God's Arsenal

Speaking of weapons takes me back to an experience in my early teens. I had a mentor who handcrafted his own hunting bows. It took a considerable amount of "convincing" for Hank to finally invite me into his shop to make a bow of my own. After hours of painstaking labor the big day finally arrived; it was time to test my new weapon.

Hank recommended I test my bow on a bale of straw, but I didn't want anything to delay my "field testing," so I substituted my mom's cedar picnic table. I flipped over the table and placed my target near the top. Drawing the arrow to full length, I took aim and released the feathered projectile. The shot went high and to the right, missing the target, and instead splitting one of the two-by-four cedar planks.

I ran up to the table and stood dumbfounded. The force of the mostly-blunt practice arrow had completely splintered the two by four, driving ten inches of my arrow through the table. It was a visceral lesson in weaponry; I had no doubt that the bow in my hands was a lethal weapon.

My life-long journey with the combination of stick and string was now vindicated; what I had first seen in a B-rated cowboy movie was now in living-color right before my eyes.

More importantly, it illustrated what awaits *anyone* who sets their hearts on *praying the Scriptures*. Learning to combine your voice and the written Word as you pray is a powerful weapon. This combination will multiply both the effectiveness and enjoyment of your prayer life.

Over the past decade, I've found I *can't* go back to simply reading the Scriptures. Instead, I always feel compelled to pray the Scriptures. The Scriptures and prayer are indivisible.

If you want joy in prayer, and if you want God's ALL, choose a life of prayer that joins God's written word with your spoken words.

Why not start right now? You will be so glad you did!

* * * * *

A Scripture-based Interactive Prayer from Psalm 19:7-12

When I hold my Bible and open it up, I thank you, Lord, that it is perfect in every way. I know I can trust the Scriptures through and through. Your words restore my soul, imparting wisdom and bringing much joy to my heart. I love Your words, which are sweeter than honey and more valuable than a treasure chest full of gold. By your Spirit, use the Scriptures to examine and purify my heart, and then fill me with your Spirit. I pray this with deep gratitude in Jesus' name, Amen.

Getting ALL In!

1. **Every time we read the Scriptures,** it's an interactive opportunity for us to pray the verses back to God. So, take a minute to look up one of your favorite Scriptures. A shorter passage might work best, but it's your choice.

2. **Read your Scripture passage aloud once or twice.** In your own words below, summarize what your Scripture passage says. Full sentences are fine, but you may want to jot down brief bullet points. Either way, you have plenty of room below.

3. **Now, pray your Scripture passage back to God.** Don't worry if you need to pause, and don't worry about saying something wrong. After all, you're simply speaking God's words back to Him. Remember Jamal from *Finding Forrester*? What you're doing may seem awkward, but the fact is you're on a well-tested path that leads to a prayer life energized by the very power of God.

There's More!

Please visit RickDPadgett.com where you'll find interactive online content and bonus articles related to the chapters in *Get Prayer and Get It All*.

9

GET PRAYER AND
GET VISION

I choose a life of prayer because it is the only way
to escape the short-sighted trap of a temporal life.

Sixth grade was my Year of Jubilee. After seven years of laboring in the brick house that was our local elementary school, I was set free—released from grade-school bondage to the halls of Junior High. In retrospect, it probably wasn't that great of a trade, but at the time it seemed like a big deal. Our final act of sixth grade triumph was outdoor school at the hallowed cabins of Camp Wygoyhum. Stealing away from parents and teachers for a whole week powerfully affirmed that I had finally "arrived." When I did arrive I found a mostly worn-out cluster of cabins leaning toward a shallow swampy lake. To me it was the Promised Land.

A torrent of giddy sixth graders burst out the school-bus doors, ready to embrace the week's adventure. The flood quickly dispersed into a scattering of gender-specific cabins, our new "home" for that week. On entering the boys' cabins our eyes were drawn to the exposed beams, tattooed with signatures and wise sayings from previous campers. Instinctively, every boy chose a bare patch of wood where he vowed to leave his mark. We also vowed to exercise our newly acquired freedom at every opportunity.

We kept the rhythm of the week through planned activities, really bad food, and pranks on unsuspecting neighbors. Our camp counselors were also students, high school volunteers returning to Camp Wygoyhum, the hallowed ground of their earlier youth. They counseled us in one important life skill: how to flirt with members of the opposite sex. Scores of 12-year-old boys took mental notes with the speed and attention of skilled courtroom stenographers.

I soon learned that the *guy* counselors planned this return to Camp Wygoyhum to be with the *girl* counselors. In a sort-of "second honeymoon," we observed our counselors belated attempts to renew the interests of female counselors who had barely noticed them in their prior sixth-grade life. Their zeal to make up for lost opportunities was a constant source of amusement.

Unexpected Life Lesson

One of highlights of the week was a midnight hike built around a lesson in astronomy. It happened to be a coed event, so I'm pretty sure the Camp director received a large sum of money from his young male volunteers. They must have paid the weather man as well because we actually had clear skies. You can imagine the bravado and giggling that accompanied our troop as we set off with flashlights blazing into the darkness.

After leaving behind the weak glow of the cabin porch lights, a cacophony of sound effects accompanied our journey. The late hour and darkness sharpened our hearing and created a nearly perfect sound stage. Wild animal hoots and calls and other less-savory selections filled everyone's ears.

We arrived at a small clearing to hear a short talk on astronomy. The first task, however, was to herd this band of "wildlife" into a circle and quiet their sound effect artistry. Every time our director managed to capture a moment of silence, the temptation to perform would overwhelm one of the sound artists. A few substantial threats and flashlight interrogations finally stifled the performances.

After a short unintelligible speech on astronomy, our counselor did something I will never forget. He tricked us into paying attention with a challenge: "Before you head back to your cabins," he commanded, "I want everyone to look up and choose your own star. Choose the brightest one you can find and keep your eyes on that star until I say it's time to look away."

Just 20 or 30 seconds later, murmurs arose from the assembled rabble. The counselor asked us to describe what we saw. A few rapt voices spoke up from the darkness. Each one explained the same phenomenon: that all the surrounding stars seemed to disappear except their chosen star.

The counselor said something inane like, "the star is responding to the fact that you have chosen it as your very own." It wasn't the real explanation, mostly because the counselor wasn't even thinking about stars when he made it up. I squinted toward him in the darkness, only to find him gazing at a female "star" the whole time he was talking.

It was a long time before I heard a real explanation of what made the other stars disappear. It has nothing to do with astronomy and everything to do with the amazing design of the human eye. Apparently, under certain circumstances, our eyes can willfully shut off their peripheral vision. That is an intriguing ability for a young counselor who "has his eye on" a girl, but it is even more intriguing when we see it as a clue to what the Scriptures say about our eyes.

Matthew 6 points to the critical importance of our eyes.

> *The eye is the lamp of the body. If your eyes are healthy, your whole body will be full of light. But if your eyes are unhealthy, your whole body will be full of darkness. If then the light within you is darkness, how great is that darkness! No one can serve two masters. Either you will hate the one and love the other, or you will be devoted to the one and despise the other (Matthew 6:22-24).*

Not only does Jesus speak out on the importance of having "healthy eyes," but His summary of choosing one "master" makes perfect sense when I reflect on the Camp Wygoyhum lesson.

Jesus teaches that the eye does two things at the same time. It not only sees, but has the ability to see in a way that chooses a singular master.

So, is the fact that our physical eye is able to exclude distractions an important clue to how things work in the spiritual realm?

Starting with Matthew 6, I searched the Scriptures for other clues. What I found was long list of references to words such as *fix, set, behold*, and *gaze*—all of which point the eye's ability to eliminate any peripheral competition. I started to realize I was on to something.

Beholding and Becoming

As I studied the many biblical references to our eyes, two things came into clear focus for me.

First, our physical eyes have a critical role to play, but we also have inner eyes of the heart.

> *When the woman **saw** that the fruit of the tree was good for food and pleasing to the eye, and also **desirable** for gaining wisdom, she took some and ate it (Genesis 3:6a).*

> *I pray that **the eyes of your heart** may be **enlightened** in order that you may know the hope to which he has called you, the riches of his glorious inheritance in his holy people, and his incomparably great power for us who believe (Ephesians 1:18-19).*

Second, the object of our gaze, both physically and in the heart, has the power to define us. It has the power to define what we value and ultimately what we do. In this sense, our eyes choose the object of our worship and transform us into that object's servants (Matthew 6:24). A friend of mine has aptly called this "beholding and becoming."

"Beholding and becoming" can be a deadly liability—if our eyes choose idolatry. At the same time, if our eyes are fixed on the one true God, creator of heaven and earth, it can be a wonderful transformational experience.

> One thing I ask from the LORD, this only do I seek: that I may dwell in the house of the LORD all the days of my life, to **gaze on the beauty of the LORD** and to seek him in his temple (Psalm 27:4).

> **Watch and pray** so that you will not fall into temptation. The spirit is willing, but the flesh is weak (Matthew 26:41, Mark 14:38; see also Luke 21:36).

> So we **fix our eyes** not on what is seen, but on **what is unseen, since** what is seen is temporary, but **what is unseen is eternal** (2 Corinthians 4:18).

These and other Scriptures convinced me to greatly value the skill of a fixed gaze and hard focus. So, how do you and I begin to practice this skill?

Scripture as a Picture Book

To find my answer I had to rethink the way I approached the Scriptures. I had always approached the Bible as God's Word, as a critical source of information, and with a sense of worship and devotion. I had learned how the various literary genres in Scripture communicate truth to us in different ways based on certain established literary principles, guidelines, and regulations. As a diligent student I actively sought to "rightly divide the word of truth."

The problem with this approach? It didn't help me answer the question raised repeatedly in Scripture itself about *how to use my eyes.*

The solution crystallized during my study. I discovered a new category within Scripture. I found that certain Scripture passages are highly visual and designed by God to "catch our eye." Some are very personal; some are the common property of all believers. All of them are designed to be accessed through the simple exercise of fixing our gaze. As this list of passages grew, I started a new Bible study file and titled it *"The Icons of Scripture."*

I began praying with these "Icons of Scripture." As I practiced this new approach, the process of "seeing" required two skills. *Seeing* not only required that I choose a scriptural focus, but also that I give myself permission to engage my imagination and invite the Holy Spirit to spark this imaginative process. I need the Holy Spirit to open my eyes to see what I am supposed to see.

For example, instead of trying to **understand** all the details of the Second Coming intellectually, I simply tried to imagine what it will look like when Jesus Christ returns. I intentionally asked the Holy Spirit to help me "see." The experience was like opening the windows of my heart on the first warm day of spring. The seeds I had planted through years of careful Bible study suddenly began to explode into a colorful bloom and I experienced a new range of emotions in prayer.

In addition to my private experiments, I began to invite some of my close friends to join me for group exercises in *icon gazing*—taking a highly visual passage of Scripture, reading it aloud, and asking the Holy Spirit to help us picture it in our mind's eye as we prayed. In one experiment we prayed through the seven days of Creation, verse by verse. It took us more than two years. We simply never got tired of seeing new things as we gathered weekly, encouraging one another to "see" what God was doing in the Creation week.

One important caveat bears mention. This exercise of gazing through Scripture can get off-track if it is ever separated from the whole counsel of Scripture. I am not advocating that anyone impose what they "see" as authoritative or new revelation without regard to the rest of Scripture. Yet in all the years we have practiced this approach to prayer and the Icons of Scripture, we have never encountered this problem. In fact the opposite is true; the Holy Spirit has used "gazing" to lead us into a deeper understanding and commitment to His *written* Word.

Before I close, I want to connect the importance of a "fixed gaze" and the main theme of this book—getting God's ALL.

In Chapter 2, I presented the idea that by simply using the *Common Laws of Love* we could come to a meaningful understanding of the First Commandment. Not only does this approach pass the litmus test of life experience and Jesus' example, but it also provides a meaningful model for the life of prayer.

Singular vision, or *fixed gaze,* is the fourth common law of love: the desire to see and be seen, as well as to see what others don't see. By taking this element of *common love* and joining it to the *icons of Scripture,* I discovered a doorway into the other three elements of love.

Developing the skill of *seeing* with my heart has become my main strategy for sustaining tangible experiences of being *with* God, for sharing joys and sorrows, and for hearing His voice in powerful and compelling ways.

When I think back to the night hike in sixth grade, the discovery that my physical eyes could choose an ALL-focus, I had no idea that God was planting a principle that would revolutionize my spiritual journey. I had no idea that God could use an optical fact to open my eyes to spiritual truth—the truth that a simple, even childlike exercise, can release me from a limited, fractured existence into the unexplored territory of God's ALL.

When we make the simple childlike decision to fix our gaze on the pictures in God's Word, we water our "seed collection" (years of careful Bible study) and then can watch it grow into colorful bloom. The Holy Spirit does the work.

In prayer, you can choose to fix your eyes on the icons God Himself has given us until they fill your vision, direct your heart, and transform your life.

What could be more exciting?

Are you ready to begin?

* * * * *

A Scripture-based Interactive Prayer from Psalm 27:4

God, I come to you and echo David's request: I want to ask You for one thing. I long to see You and fix my eyes on You. You are beautiful. You fill my heart's desire for beauty. My eyes were made for this one thing: to see You. I am standing in Your temple, watching for You to empower my offering of worship. I ask that I may live in Your house as Your son/daughter all the days of my life. I picture myself walking into the doors of Your house and never leaving. Every day that I awake, I awake in my Father's house. Every night I fall asleep with You. Show me more and more how what my eyes see is the key awakening my heart to be a lover.

Getting ALL In!

1. **Hebrews 12:2 tells us the secret to perseverance is** "fixing our eyes on Jesus." What tool or icon can you use to set your eyes on Jesus Christ? To begin, you may want to find a Scripture passage that describes Jesus

in ways that will help you meditate on His beauty. A favorite passage for many is Matthew 11:28-29.

2. **Psalm 115:4-8 says something rather startling:** the object of our worship will conform us into its image. Again, this the principle of "beholding and becoming." In the space below, make two lists. On the left, list the characteristics of idols. On the right, list how the one true God, creator of heaven and earth, is vastly different.

IDOLS ARE...   GOD IS...

3. **In Psalm 23 David says that God** "Prepares a table in the presence of my enemies." Do you think this kind of rest and confidence is connected to the fixed gaze of worship? If so, how important is "seeing" when we encounter difficulty and even spiritual opposition?

There's More!

Please visit RickDPadgett.com where you'll find interactive online content and bonus articles related to the chapters in *Get Prayer and Get It All*.

10

GET PRAYER AND GET
YOUR BROTHERS AND SISTERS

*I choose a life of prayer because it is the
foundation of unity with my brothers and sisters.*

Early in my life I caught the fishing disease. It took deep root in my bones
and I am now beyond the reach of any cure. One symptom of my sad estate is
the delusion that everyone should fish. As a result of this delusion, countless
non-fishing friends have been the subject of my efforts to cure their lack of zeal
for catching fish.

At one point I was gripped by this evangelistic compulsion on behalf of a man
I loved and respected, with one outstanding exception: he didn't fish. I baited
him with pictures of my success and leveraged his wife's appetite for fresh
salmon. Finally he came to the net, I scooped him up, dropped him in my
boat, and we went out for a day of fishing. At every opportunity I pointed out
the beauty and mystery of fishing, but by mid-morning a dark cloud hung over
our morning that smelled like skunk. We had no fish.

Then it happened. My friend's rod began to jerk violently and he was fast onto
a salmon—a big one. Between the swift currents of the Columbia River and
the heavy fish, my friend saw what looked like miles of fishing line tear off the
reel. Even my novice friend knew this was no ordinary salmon. A good while
passed before the fish left off the deep runs and turned to close range tactics,
head shaking and body rolling. But still the hook held and the big fish finally
ran out of reserves. I steered the boat out of the main current and in one glorious scoop of triumph, I netted my friend's first salmon: thirty-four pounds of
bright Chinook flopping in the back of my boat.

Hand slapping, pictures, and whooping followed. The picture of my friend
holding his prize fish shows his epic smile. He used my large ice chest to trans-
port the salmon home and show off to his family and friends. Everyone who
saw the fish or the pictures was in awe of our success: the perfect first day of
salmon fishing.

There was just one problem. My convert never returned for his next lesson.

Although he lives nearby and the river is ever present, the fever never transferred to my friend. He had been there, done that, it was nice, and he has moved on. He never returned for an encore. Apparently the guy was immune to the fishing virus. I could only shrug and go looking for another unsuspecting and uninitiated fisherman.

Being Hooked by a Deeper Longing

I tell this story because I love fish stories, but also because it illustrates a critical part of my faith journey.

As a brand-new believer I too had a moment of beginner's luck. My very first church experience was shaped by a rare group of people who had captured the prize of authentic community. They enjoyed being together in a way that was contagious. I seized every opportunity to be with these people. I was a new Christian with no church background, yet I had been born into this Christian fellowship as my first church experience. I had no clue how rare and valuable this experience was; I was even less aware it was foreign to many Christians. In a sense, I was the novice fisherman holding my thirty-four pound salmon, oblivious that most fishermen never catch such a prize.

I now understand quite clearly that my first church experience *could have* pointed my life in any of three different directions. It could have simply been a "nice" experience, to add to my list of other "nice" experiences. It could have ended in a major disappointment, causing me to forsake Christian community as so many others do. Or, it could have been a *transformational* experience, forever changing my life and marking me with a longing for authentic community. In God's kindness it became the latter. At the time, I didn't even realize it, but my initial experience of authentic Christian community deeply imprinted itself on my life. I have been seeking encores ever since.

The Hook of Longing Goes Even Deeper

In God's wisdom, after this initial impression of authentic community, I went into a desert of isolation. Through college and early marriage, and the initial years of ministry, I always longed for that first experience of community.

In 2003 all that changed. Like most big moments in my life, I didn't see it coming.

It started as a simple experiment—just me and one other man meeting to pray together. We had only two controlling ideas: that we needed to meet together weekly, and that our conversation should be both horizontal and vertical. We also based every week's prayer and conversation around a passage of Scripture.

My friend and I started a yearly Bible reading program and found that reading the same Scriptures apart helped us find a Scripture focus in our weekly times together.

With these simple tools in hand we launched out. We met weekly, building our conversation with each other and God on a specific passage of Scripture. This was not a Bible study or a prayer meeting, both of which set an agenda. Instead, we inquired of God during our meeting: not insisting on our questions, but rather making room for **His** questions.

In the context of this simple exercise something began to happen that went beyond our limited experience and expectations. This regular, intentional, structured, and yet open agenda made a place for God to show up. It seemed to attract the Holy Spirit's attention. I was often reminded of His promise, "For where two or three gather in my name, there am I with them" (Matthew 18:20).

Not only did God show up. More people showed up. It was uncomfortable at times, especially when visitors showed up expecting a scheduled format. Then again, the rewards were huge. As God invaded our little gathering, isolation left us. In every meeting, it became obvious that God knew our hearts, and that emboldened us to share our hearts with each other. After living in a wilderness, we found the gift of authentic Christ-centered community being restored to our lives. I often have called this, "The best part of my week."

We named ourselves Forge 218, after Genesis 2:18, which says, "The Lord God said, 'It is not good for the man to be alone.'" We, like Adam, were learning that even in the most beautiful surroundings, we were not created for isolation.

Forge 218 continues to this day, operating under the same simple rules. For more than a decade it has been a well of life to all who participate. It also happens to be where I discovered everything I now teach about prayer.

The Longing Becomes My Teacher

After years of longing, I discovered that simple authentic corporate prayer is God's strategy for us to experience His ALL with our brothers and sisters in Christ. As a result of my earlier desert experience, I have learned to compare its simplicity to manna, to thank God for it, and enjoy it for what it is—bread from heaven.

Forge 218 has now piled up years of sustained community built on this model. The model is both embarrassingly easy and profoundly important. We had stumbled onto the secret to the Second Commandment. We took this commandment out of the theory box and turned it into a living demonstration. The simple strategy of building prayer-centered community has transformed our relationships with brothers and sisters, empowering us to be both lovers of God and lovers of His people.

When prayer and obedience to the First and Second Commandment are joined together, you and I will witness God's power and understand why the Lord said, "It is not good for man to be alone."

Among other things, it will help us practice the Four Common Laws of Love with God and with one another: (1) being together, (2) setting our eyes on one another and God's Word, (3) hearing one another's voice, and (4) sharing joys and sorrows.

Although those of us in Forge 218 are still learning to put all of this into practice, I would like to offer the following observations gleaned from our journey so far.

Observations on Building a Prayer-centered Community

Root vs. Fruit

The life of any plant is in the root. It is the first thing that appears when the life inside the seed is awakened. If the root fails to connect to the soil, life stalls and all potential is lost. Although roots are first, they are not very appealing; they do their best work in hiding. Fruit, on the other hand, is everyone's favorite. Looks good, tastes good, and it conveniently fits in your pocket. It is easy to like fruit. In a real sense, the roots do all the dirty work and the fruit gets all the love. But the life of the plant is anchored in the root. Fruit is clear proof that the root is doing its job.

The relationship between the root and the fruit illustrates the fundamental tension that exists between the First and Second Commandment. Loving God is clearly our starting point. It is the root of our life. Yet loving people is the fruit of our love for God. It's how we know we are truly rooted in our love for God.

Loving God is where all of life starts. The "fruit" of loving our brothers and sisters apart from the root of loving God is a recipe for frustration and failure.

While the voice of human need constantly demands that we authenticate our faith by responding to visible circumstances, it is never God's plan that we allow these demands to usurp His place as the center of our affections. As a result, there will always be a fundamental tension between the First and Second Commandments as you try to live them out.

Consider the most explicit teaching Jesus ever gave on the Second Commandment—the story of the Good Samaritan. The Samaritan was a religious outcast, yet was commended by Jesus for loving his neighbor after the "respected" priest and Levite missed the mark. Their excuse for not loving their neighbor? They were too preoccupied with getting to the Temple, ostensibly to perform their First Commandment duties.

The Samaritan illustrates one side of the tension, while John's letter to the church of Ephesus reveals the other. The Church at Ephesus dutifully modeled Second Commandment obedience. They labored in the midst of persecution and false doctrine and did not growing weary of doing good. And yet Jesus gave them a stern warning, telling them to return to their "first love" (Revelation 2:4).

In both cases, Jesus puts His finger on our propensity for getting things turned around. While the First Commandment must go first, the Second Commandment *must* follow. And while the Second Commandment is important, it must draw its life from loving God.

The bottom line? In the midst of all the demands of life, I have to keep reminding myself, *the kindest thing I can do for another human being is to be a lover of God. It is the highest service I can offer to my fellow man.*

To put it another way, if we make community our primary goal, we lose twice. We will fail at both the First and Second Commandments, resulting in isolation from God and people. On the other hand, if we resolutely fix our eyes on the primary task of loving God, constantly checking our lives by this gold standard, then we can also obtain the prize of community. Authentic pursuit of the First Commandment always empowers us to obey the Second Commandment.

Let's turn our focus, then, to the question of obeying the Second Commandment.

I will focus on some key markers that distinguish authentic community, "proofs" that our relationships are built on the First and Second Commandments in tandem. These are *culture indicators* of healthy Christian community, and visible evidence of the corporate life God intended. When the roots are at work, everyone, including God, can enjoy the fruit.

Fruit #1: Unity

When God picks up His produce basket and takes a stroll through the orchard of His Church, one of the first things to catch His eye is the fruit of unity. *Unity describes how the Father, the Son, and the Holy Spirit love each other* and why we call their relationship a tri-unity or Trinity. When our relationships are connected to the perfect community of the Father, the Son, and the Holy Spirit, we are displaying the centerpiece of God's beauty.

How valuable is unity to God? It was one of the last things Jesus prayed for prior to His death (John 17:20-26). Anyone who sabotages unity is literally detestable to God (Proverbs 6:19), while His anointing and blessing land where unity is demonstrated among God's people (Psalm 133). One of the most startling things about unity is that it is an evangelistic tool. Jesus said the answer to His prayer for unity would demonstrate the Gospel to an unbelieving world (John 17:23). Clearly, when individuals unite in a corporate response to God, it sets the stage for a multitude of good things.

Fruit #2 and #3: Identity and Worship

What else is God looking for when He strolls through the orchard of His Church? He is looking for people who know how to live in their identity. **Our true identity is sourced in God's claim on our life.** When God stakes His claim, it subordinates every other attempt to possess our lives.

We see this power behind a number of "My" and "Mine" declarations of the Lord.

The two most famous:

- To Pharaoh, "Let **My** people go."

- To Jesus, "You are **My** Son."

When God says "Mine," it means we are wanted, that we belong. God's declaration of "Mine" also says we are chosen, then invited—and mostly, that we are loved. God's name is even marked on us when we are baptized "in the name" of the Father, the Son and Holy Spirit. The greatest claim of ownership and belonging is to bear someone's name.

So, what's the connection between identity and worship? While identity is the confident understanding of who we are, worship is the confident understanding of who God is. We are made to respond in worship when God reveals His identity to us—in other words, when we understand who God is.

Authentic Christian community draws its life from corporate agreement about our identity and about the reason to worship. This *unity* takes place when confidence grows and matures between God and His people. It is never static. On one hand, we delight in our identity as His treasured possession, sons and daughters who are cherished and loved. On the other hand, we keep learning of God's character through personal encounters and we respond in whole-hearted worship.

As we walk with confidence of His claim on our lives (sure identity) and respond in worship to Him, we see that these two realities (identity and worship) are the Holy Spirit's predominant work. First, He facilitates worship in agreement with the truth of who God is (John 4:23-24); and second, He is the *Spirit of adoption* who helps us to agree with God about our own identity (Romans 8:14-17).

Fruit #4: Wisdom

As God stops to examine the orchard of His Church, He is always looking for one of His favorite fruits: wisdom. It is not exclusive to the New Testament Church, but we are supposed to take it to a new level.

Wisdom has been defined as the ability to judge life outside the immediate tyranny of the clock. Wisdom is the inner eco-system of the person who has connected with eternity. In contrast, the person who is not connected with eternity lives in folly, and is called a fool.

The only way to get wisdom is to put God first. Wisdom paraphrases the First Commandment by saying, "The fear of the Lord is the beginning of wisdom." If you try to do the Second Commandment first, you get something quite different: The fear of man is the making of a fool.

Although wisdom is founded in the First Commandment, it is very good for Second Commandment relationships. In fact, it's hard to imagine loving my neighbor if I am living in the death spiral of folly.

Not surprisingly, wisdom grows in close proximity to unity, identity, and worship. They were meant to be together. One key distinctive of unity, identity, and worship is that they also operate outside the temporal realm. They are "off the clock." In this sense each of them is in sync with wisdom.

For example, if you are wise, you will be a worshipper. But it is also true that if you are a worshipper, you will become wise. They work together. Obviously, since unity is sourced in the Trinity, unity also requires an exit from the constraints of the hour glass. The same is true with identity.

I have found it very helpful and important to draw a line between my eternal identity and my temporary assignments. On the eternal identity side, I have three things written: son, priest, and bride. These three will last forever.

On the temporary assignments side, I have a multitude of task-oriented things that fill my life. Although I can do things within those tasks that will connect to eternity, none of them create value, security, or identity. So, I call these temporal roles. Roles are good as long as they stay on their side of the line. If they try to cross over to the other side, I smack them with a rolled up newspaper. I call that practical wisdom!

Lots of other trees grow in the orchard of God's church, but I chose these to illustrate the main point of this chapter and actually of this book.

Carefully read these next few sentences.

- Pursuing the First Commandment wholeheartedly is prerequisite for good, positive, healthy Second Commandment relationships.

- If loving God is the primary aspiration of my life, I will be well equipped to love my neighbor.

- The best thing I can do for my brothers and sisters is to be a lover of God.

How to Develop a Corporate Prayer Life that Builds Up the Church

Prayer is a fundamental exercise in nurturing authentic Christian community. It is the First Commandment root from which the orchard of God's Church will grow the fruit of unity, identity, worship, and wisdom. Many prayers in Scripture specifically ask for these realities, telling me that it is God's will that we experience local church community life blessed by these fruit. It also tells me that if I don't ask for them, there is a good chance I will not enjoy them.

The question before us is: *How do we begin to develop corporate prayer that exercises and nourishes the Body of Jesus Christ so it can demonstrate healthy community?*

I would like to summarize my answer to that important question, and then move directly into an interactive exercise based on these principles.

1. Start with the written Word.

Choose a prayer facilitator whose main task is to choose a Scripture and keep the meeting tracking in that passage. Ideally, the passage should contain between one and eight verses, and be fairly simple and straightforward in its focus.

2. Ask your team, "What does this passage say about God?"

Use the voice of declaration and thanksgiving to respond to God based on what you see in the Scripture passage. If you have a seasoned musician/singer in your group, he or she may be able to help with this, but it isn't essential. Just use your voice and your body to declare and celebrate who God is—for He is worthy!

3. Ask your team, "What does this Scripture say about us?"

Start with declaration and celebration, but leave room for confession. In this part we begin to see the contradictions between what God says about us and what we or our circumstances say. If things get bogged down here, go back to #2.

4. After you have traveled through steps 1-3, start to intercede.

Intercession means closing the gap. The facilitator wants to keep this moving and focused on "we/us" instead of "I/me" or "they/them." He or she also wants to safeguard against whining or backdoor criticism. If things get off track, again go back to #2.

5. Invite prayer for individuals.

Often by this point the group members already have been ministered to each other by doing this interactive exercise together, and therefore may want less time for individual attention. Putting this step toward the end also keeps individuals from hijacking the gathering. Individual ministry is the biggest derailleur of corporate prayer.

6. Conclude with a brief review of what has happened.

This is easier if you use a whiteboard as you go through steps 1 to 5. If someone likes to write, you can ask them to keep a corporate journal as well.

I have used this basic model for hundreds of corporate prayer meetings. It has proven invaluable. You can add other steps, but this basic model is so easy anyone can do it.

Give it a try!

* * * * *

A Scripture-based Prayer for Joining the First and Second Commandments as an Expression of Supernatural Unity

Listen as Jesus prays for us...

> *My prayer is not for them alone. I pray also for those who will believe in me through their message, that all of them may be one, Father, just as you are in me and I am in you. May they also be in us so that the world may believe that you sent me. I have given them the glory that you gave me, that they may be one as we are one—I in them and you in me—so they may be brought to complete unity. Then the world will know that you sent me and have loved them even as you have loved me. Father, I want those you have given me to be with me where I am, and to see my glory, the glory you have given me because you loved me before the creation of the world. Righteous Father, though the world does not know you, I know you, and they know that you have sent me. I have made you known to them, and will continue to make you known in order that the love you have for me may be in them and that I myself may be in them (John 17:20-26).*

Getting ALL In!

1. **When you think of "fruit" in the context of a Christian life,** what is the first thing that comes to mind? Is your first response to measure fruit as an individual's responsibility or as our corporate responsibility? Why is this such an important question?

2. **When Jesus gave the disciples a model prayer in Matthew 6,** He started with the word "Our." What does that tell us about prayer and our fellow believers?

3. **Jesus also taught about the importance of secret prayer.** Do you think He intended that we should always pray alone? What was His example? What was the practice of the early Church in the book of Acts?

4. **How important is it for families to discover a way to pray together?** Have you had a positive experience of praying with your earthly family? How could the skills learned in Chapters 8 and 9 help us do this better?

5. **How important is it that communities of believers pray together?** Have you had a positive experience praying with your church family? Have you ever been part of a prayer gathering that met together on a regular basis? How could the skills of Chapter 8 and 9 help in this context?

11

GET PRAYER AND
GET THE LOST

I choose a life of prayer because it is the only way to receive and then share God's mercy with those who are lost.

When I was seven years old my family moved to a new neighborhood. According to local bratty boy protocol, initiation into the new tribe required that I fight a member in good standing. The fight was arranged when one of the older boys stole my football. The rule was simple: if you want the football and tribal privileges, you had to fight to prove your worthiness. It was a sticky situation. Losing your honor at the starting line would not bode well for what was to follow.

At the last minute I was rescued when my two older brothers intervened and the rabble leader backed down. My opponent and I were so relieved by this graceful escape that we became fast friends. Little did I know that this un-neighborly encounter would set the stage for the greatest gift of my life.

A few months after meeting my new friend, tragedy struck their family. His mom was involved in a head-on collision that killed the other driver and left her hanging on to life by a thread. The doctor called the family together and told them things looked very grim. All they could do was wait.

Days turned to weeks and my friend's mom hung on despite the dismal odds. She eventually left the hospital, but would never be the same woman. Her body was bent by the encounter, and a sort of crookedness stuck to her appearance. As bad as that was, the doctors insisted the long and heavy front end of her 1960s Cadillac spared her from a much worse fate.

The physical consequences of the wreck, however, were not the biggest changes that visited her life. Somewhere in her journey through the physical extremes of this experience, my friend's mom acquired a completely new dimension of her faith in God.

Before the wreck, this woman was a casual believer. After the wreck, her life burned with the fire of eternity. I think she must have come very close to glory.

Remember, through all these changes, her son and I were still pre-adolescent boys. Eternity wasn't even on our radar. We were still under the strong delusion of our own immortality, meaning life at my friend's house became a clash of cultures. I spent a lot of time there and trust me, things could get ugly.

One of the biggest rubs was this woman's audacity to claim that in prayer God would speak to her, and even worse that He would speak to her about me. I remember being so exasperated that I blurted out, "Ruth, if God had something to say about my life, why doesn't He just tell me about it?"

She would look at me with her crooked stare, smile, and head down the hallway to her bedroom. Of course, I found this infuriating, but she just kept smiling.

A few years later things with Ruth came to a crisis. I was out with a friend when the front tire of the car we were riding hit a soft shoulder and careened out of control. It smashed full tilt into a huge maple tree. The tree didn't budge. My face hit something and I lost a bunch of teeth and a fair amount of blood. The dentist put the teeth back where they belonged and, to make sure they stayed put, he wired my mouth shut. Add facial stitches and bruises to complete the picture. I wasn't a pretty sight.

The first place I went after getting back on my feet was my friend's house. I came through the back door unannounced and ran straight into Ruth. She fixed her crooked stare on me with unusual ferocity. She didn't say hello or inquire about my health. She just said, "He was right, you're gonna be okay. He said He is not finished with you yet."

With this she spun around and headed down the hallway. My mouth was wired shut so I couldn't say anything even if I wanted to.

I always think about this moment when I read the story of Zacharias, father of John the Baptist. Sometimes God just doesn't want to hear any more stupid.

* * * * *

Less than two years after this exchange between fellow crash survivors, I had another collision. This time it wasn't a car wreck; it was a collision with God. The mercy that Ruth had received, which she had breathed on me, suddenly overtook my life. And not only mine, but many others, including almost every young man who had been part of our original pack of bratty boys.

Less than six months after my conversion to the God of Ruth, I sat in her front room with fifty other young people, most of us new converts. We were there to sing, pray, and study the Scriptures.

Ruth would occasionally peek around the corner and watch the proceedings. She was witnessing the multiplication of her mercy encounter with Jesus. She never admitted it, but I think the answers to her prayers even caught her off guard.

Ruth's life experience of mercy and the prayers she breathed on those around her remain my greatest example of someone living out obedience to these words:

> First of all, then, I urge that entreaties and prayers, petitions and thanks-givings, be made on behalf of all men… This is good and acceptable in the sight of **God our Savior, who desires all men to be saved** and to come to the knowledge of the truth. For there is one God, and one mediator also between God and men, the man Christ Jesus, who gave Himself as a ransom for all… Therefore I want the men in every place to pray, lifting up holy hands, without wrath and dissension (1 Timothy 2:1-8).

Mercy and God's ALL

I tell this story to underline the vast dimensions of *mercy*. It is a mega member of God's ALL vocabulary, especially when turned into prayer.

It is important that mercy stays connected to God's ALL, however, because mercy is such a lopsided word. For you to receive mercy means *you don't get what you do deserve*. For you to extend mercy means you withhold the judgment that someone deserves. By implication, the *mercy giver* is assuming another person's debt. No one can sustain mercy on their own—without God's ALL working through them.

If you haven't received mercy, you won't be able to share it. That is why mercy always must be directly linked to God's provision, especially through a life of sustained prayer. Prayer is where we find mercy!

> Let us then approach God's throne of grace with confidence, so that we may receive **mercy** and **find** grace to help us in our time of need. (Hebrews 4:16)

When we join mercy with a voice of prayer, we position ourselves to partner with God as He leads people in their own Exodus out of unbelief and into His mercy by faith.

Another requirement for extending mercy to an unbeliever is remembering our own mercy encounter. This is the simple secret behind Ruth's example. To love someone mired in debt, we must remember we had our own turn in the pit. We must actually see ourselves in that person.

This is part of what Jesus meant when He said, "Love your neighbor as yourself." In another passage He emphasizes this by saying, "The one who is forgiven much, loves much" (Luke 7:41).

Some of us never get over our mercy encounter. This is how it should be! Jesus said the merciful are blessed, because they will continue to receive more mercy (Matthew 5:7). If we want to love unbelievers, we have to be *mercy multipliers*. We use the mercy we have received as God's tool to mid-wife people through experiences of desperation.

Always remember, your accreditation to mid-wife others is that you have already been through the process. As a follower of Jesus, you already are working with the greatest mercy multiplier in human history.

The Mercies of God

We see God at work in a number of New Testament conversions. These are examples of God partnering with His people to extend the boundaries of mercy and mid-wife people into God's kingdom.

First, let's take a quick look at Peter's mercy encounter with Cornelius in Acts 10. Prayer is featured prominently on both ends of this particular story. While neither man really knew how to pray for mercy, they were praying to be in agreement with God's work. Peter was stuck in his Jewish limitations— unable to extend mercy and withhold judgment about who was worthy of hearing the saving message of Jesus. That is, until he prayed.

Cornelius was a god-fearing Roman, eager to please God but ignorant about Jesus Christ. He had a deep longing to receive mercy, but didn't know where to find it. That is, until he prayed.

The wonderful ending to this story is that God's relentless mercy breaks through in spite of Cornelius and Peter's limitations, in answer to their disciplined times in prayer. This is encouraging for those who tend to feel inadequate.

The second story is **Philip's mercy encounter with the Ethiopian eunuch** (Acts 8). Philip had a unique angle on God's mercy. It was shaped in part by his experience of being persecuted. Philip's close associate, Stephen, had been brutally martyred.

Despite being on the run from the trouble at Jerusalem, Philip connected with the teachings of Jesus about responding in mercy. He was gifted as an evangelist (Acts 21:8), a gifting that is particularly shaped for demonstrating mercy to those who aren't yet saved. This whole event is set in motion because Phillip had a listening ear for the Spirit's voice in the normal routine of his day. Who knows what he was doing right before he heard the Holy Spirit tell him to "Go to that chariot and stay near it." The fact is he was able to hear and respond. Philip took part in a "special delivery" of God's mercy to the longing heart of this Ethiopian eunuch.

What can we learn about mercy from Philip? First, our mercy expression is often rooted in personal trials and loss where we received mercy. Second, God loves to combine His gift of mercy with our gifting and abilities. As an extension of God's ALL, mercy multiplies our giftings. Lastly, our private life of prayer activates God's mercy to unbelievers in our public life. This trifecta of mercy miraculously moved in on the Cornelius and the Ethiopian eunuch—moving him from unbelief to faith in a dramatic fashion.

The final mercy story is considered by most to be the preeminent demonstration of mercy in the entire Bible. I am talking about the conversion of Saul the persecutor of Christians into Paul the champion of mercy.

In this case, Jesus initiated this mercy event in person. It was a Luke 6:36 message, "Be merciful, just as your Father is merciful," hand-delivered by the Master of mercy.

What can we learn from this epic mercy event?

Our first clue goes back to the stoning of Stephen. The last words out of Stephen's mouth were a mercy prayer, "Lord, do not hold this sin against them." The very next verse tells us, "And Saul was there, giving approval to his death."

It is hard not to connect Stephen's prayer to the Damascus road intervention, especially when we realize that Acts was written by Luke, Paul's close friend, for the explicit purpose of showing how Paul became connected to the Church.

Ironically, no one in the early Church had a big enough definition of mercy to even think to include Saul. It took another personal visit from Jesus, complete with arm twisting, to get a single disciple to show mercy by praying with Saul.

[10] In Damascus there was a disciple named Ananias. The Lord called to him in a vision, "Ananias!" "Yes, Lord," he answered.

*[11] The Lord told him, "Go to the house of Judas on Straight Street and ask for a man from Tarsus named Saul, **for he is praying**. [12] In a vision he has seen a man named Ananias come and place his hands on him to restore his sight."*

[17] Then Ananias went to the house and entered it. Placing his hands on Saul, he said, "Brother Saul, the Lord—Jesus, who appeared to you on the road as you were coming here—has sent me so that you may see again and be filled with the Holy Spirit." [18] Immediately, something like scales fell from Saul's eyes, and he could see again. He got up and was baptized (Acts 9:10-18).

The story line follows the familiar pattern of mercy. The partnership begins with all parties in the posture of prayer. Stephen, Paul, and Ananias navigated this mega mercy event by exercising the voice of prayer. God makes up what is lacking in the transaction by direct intervention. The result is that Jesus is revealed as the supreme demonstration of mercy in human experience. This is God's model for multiplying mercy throughout the Scriptures.

These mercy stories show how New Testament believers received mercy through prayer and then partnered with the Holy Spirit to deliver mercy to unbelievers.

So, what have we learned?

- Thankfully, God loves to exercise mercy and He doesn't give up.

- God isn't reluctant to save the worst of the worst.

- A few are mercy warriors like Stephen and my friend Ruth, but the rest of us seem to catch on only a little at a time.

- Not only does God exercise mercy, but He also relentlessly insists that we partner with Him in this ministry.

- Partnering with God in His mercy ministry always comes back to the simplicity of the life-giving conversation we call prayer. Prayer sustains mercy in our hearts, it nurtures life and authentic community among believers, and it is so powerful that it can bring life to those currently outside the family of faith.

Is There a Saul in Your Life?

It is almost as if God is saying, "Pick the least merciful person you know and begin to breathe the mercy prayer on their life. Test My mercy and see if it is bigger than anything you can ask or imagine."

Maybe God wants to partner with you to turn another Saul into another Apostle Paul. What would happen if that impossible person someday could testify to God's great mercy?

Paul's own testimony still challenges us to believe for this type of "mercy miracle."

> *Even though I was once a blasphemer and a persecutor and a violent man, I was shown mercy because I acted in ignorance and unbelief. The grace of our Lord was poured out on me abundantly, along with the faith and love that are in Christ Jesus.*
>
> *Here is a trustworthy saying that deserves full acceptance: **Christ Jesus** **came into the world to save sinners**—of whom I am the worst. But for that very reason I was shown mercy so that in me, the worst of sinners, Christ Jesus might display his unlimited patience as an example for those who would believe on him and receive eternal life.*
>
> *Now to the King eternal, immortal, invisible, the only God, be honor and glory for ever and ever. Amen (1 Timothy 1:13-17).*

* * * * *

A Scripture-based Interactive Prayer from Jude 1:20-23

Father, I surrender to Your mercy. I ask that You would remind me of the times Your great mercy has intervened in my life. Renew in me the desperate cry of "Mercy!" on behalf of my neighbors who are still outside saving faith. Give me faith to believe that You are still the God whose Gospel transforms lives here and now and for eternity. I want to partner with You in this miracle, and I know I cannot do this without learning to breath the mercy prayer over the lost. Thank You that Your mercy is new every morning, and that You are always ready to answer this prayer. In Jesus' name I pray, Amen.

Getting ALL In!

1. **Read Matthew 18:12-14.** Why would a shepherd leave his flock of sheep?

2. **Read Mark 10:45.** The Son of Man, Jesus Christ, came to do what?

3. **Read Luke 6:27-36.** In verse 31, Jesus paraphrases the Second Commandment. Is this passage about our relationship with believers or unbelievers? In verse 36, how does Jesus summarize our relationships in this context?

There's More!

Please visit RickDPadgett.com where you'll find interactive online content and bonus articles related to the chapters in *Get Prayer and Get It All*.

While you're online, I invite you to visit my Blog, Facebook page or Twitter feed.

- RickDPadgett.com/ricks-blog

- www.Facebook.com/RickDPadgett

- Twitter.com/RickDPadgett

I would love to hear from you:

- My email address, RickDPadgett@gmail.com

Thank You for Reading But...

Please don't put this book on a shelf. Instead, please share it with a family member or friend. Better yet, share copies with everyone you know!

This book comes in several convenient formats. The first is a free .pdf version you can forward via email to anyone you wish.

The second is an inexpensive trade paperback edition available for sale on

- Amazon

- BarnesandNoble.com

- BooksaMillion.com

- ChristianBook.com

- www.CreateSpace.com/4468779

- other online book retailers

Made in the USA
Charleston, SC
25 October 2013